EXCUSES BEGONE!

The Power of Intention (abridged 4-CD set)
A Promise Is a Promise (audio book)
The Secrets of the Power of Intention (6-CD set)
10 Secrets for Success and Inner Peace
There Is a Spiritual Solution to Every Problem
The Wayne Dyer Audio Collection/CD Collection
Your Journey to Enlightenment (6-tape program)

DVDs
Change Your Thoughts—Change Your Life
Inspiration
The Power of Intention
The Shift
10 Secrets for Success and Inner Peace
There's a Spiritual Solution to Every Problem

MISCELLANEOUS
Change Your Thoughts—Change Your Life Perpetual Flip Calendar
Everyday Wisdom Perpetual Flip Calendar
Inner Peace Cards
Inspiration Cards
Inspiration Perpetual Flip Calendar
The Power of Intention Cards
The Power of Intention Perpetual Flip Calendar
10 Secrets for Success and Inner Peace Cards
10 Secrets for Success and Inner Peace gift products:
Notecards, Candle, and *Journal*

All of the above are available at your local
bookstore, or may be ordered by visiting:

Hay House USA: **www.hayhouse.com®**
Hay House Australia: **www.hayhouse.com.au**
Hay House UK: **www.hayhouse.co.uk**
Hay House South Africa: **www.hayhouse.co.za**
Hay House India: **www.hayhouse.co.in**

EXCUSES BEGONE!

HOW TO CHANGE LIFELONG, SELF-DEFEATING THINKING HABITS

Dr. Wayne W. Dyer

HAY HOUSE, INC.
Carlsbad, California • New York City
London • Sydney • Johannesburg
Vancouver • Hong Kong • New Delhi

Published and distributed in the United States by: Hay House, Inc.: www.hayhouse .com • **Published and distributed in Australia by:** Hay House Australia Pty. Ltd.: www.hayhouse.com.au • **Published and distributed in the United Kingdom by:** Hay House UK, Ltd.: www.hayhouse.co.uk • **Published and distributed in the Republic of South Africa by:** Hay House SA (Pty), Ltd.: www.hayhouse.co.za • **Distributed in Canada by:** Raincoast: www.raincoast.com • **Published in India by:** Hay House Publishers India: www.hayhouse.co.in

Wayne Dyer's editor: Joanna Pyle
Editorial supervision: Jill Kramer • *Design:* Tricia Breidenthal

Library of Congress Cataloging-in-Publication Data

Dyer, Wayne W.
  Excuses begone! : how to change lifelong, self-defeating thinking habits / Wayne W. Dyer.
    p. cm.
  ISBN 978-1-4019-2173-6 (hardcover : alk. paper) 1. Thought and thinking.
2. Change (Psychology) 3. Self-actualization (Psychology) 4. Habit breaking. I. Title.
  BF441.D94 2009
  158.1--dc22   2008053700

ISBN: 978-1-4019-2173-6

12 11 10 09   5 4 3 2
1st edition, May 2009
2nd edition, May 2009

Printed in the United States of America

For Tiffany Saia.
The light from which
I *Shine On* . . .

CONTENTS

INTRODUCTION

I spent the year 2006 immersed in the ancient teachings of Lao-tzu, studying his monumental tome, the Tao Te Ching. I read, meditated, lived, and then wrote an essay on each of the 81 verses of the Tao, which many have called the wisest book ever written. That collection of essays is titled *Change Your Thoughts—Change Your Life: Living the Wisdom of the Tao*. I learned, and to this day, practice, *what* to think, although all that Lao-tzu taught me in that year is beyond my abilities to describe completely.

I find I now choose thoughts that are flexible, not rigid; soft, not hard. I think with humility, not arrogance; with detachment, not attachment. I practice thinking small and accomplishing big things, as well as thinking in harmony with nature, rather than with my ego. The idea of not interfering replaces meddling and advising. I prefer peaceful solutions over the notion of fighting to solve disputes. I opt for contentment, rather than ambition; arriving, not striving. And most significantly, I choose thoughts that are congruous with the Great Tao (God), rather than the illusions of self-importance conjured up by ego.

Excuses Begone!—the book you're presently reading—was also influenced by that eminent master Lao-tzu. Since the Tao Te Ching taught me *what* kind of thinking harmonized with my higher self, I asked Lao-tzu for advice on *how to change* long-established habits of thought. I realized that knowing what to think does not necessarily clarify how to go about changing a lifetime of habitual thinking. Thus, I've drawn on Lao-tzu's wisdom by contemplating his teachings and asking for his guidance on what it takes to bring about a change in the long-held habits of thought that manifest as excuses. Through a process of writing that felt as though I were being directed by a force larger than myself, the *Excuses Begone!* paradigm evolved with what appears to be the cooperation of this man named Lao-tzu, who lived some 2,500 years ago.

This paradigm works! I've taken many people through the seven questions that constitute this exciting new paradigm, and I've seen powerful changes take place to my—and their—delighted amazement. (I've even worked the paradigm on myself and turned some habits of thought around almost magically.) By examining the support system that individuals have erected over a long period of time, often going back to early childhood, and putting these timeworn thoughts through the seven steps in this paradigm, I find that excuses begin to fade away. They become replaced with thoughts that speak fervently, almost shouting, *Yes, you can change any excuse pattern, no matter how long or pervasive the conditioning process has been!*

I've seen men and women give up a lifetime of being overweight or addicted to all manner of substances by simply applying the principles that are inherent in the *Excuses Begone!* approach to life. If you're truly serious about changing any long-established habits of thought that have led you to use excuses as your rationale for staying the same, then I encourage you to follow the practices presented in these pages.

The great poet Rainer Maria Rilke once observed that "behind the world our names enclose is the nameless: our true archetype and home." I would add, "Behind the world your excuses describe is the Great Tao; let yourself be lived by it, and all of those excuses will fade away so that you finally come home once and for all."

— Wayne W. Dyer
Maui, Hawaii

Don't believe
everything you
think!

PART I

IDENTIFYING
AND REMOVING
HABITUAL
THINKING

*"Every human being's essential nature is perfect and
faultless, but after years of immersion in the world we
easily forget our roots and take on a counterfeit nature."*

— Lao-tzu

CHAPTER 1

YES, YOU CAN
CHANGE OLD HABITS

"I wasn't kissing her. I was whispering in her mouth."

— Chico Marx
(Response to his wife when she caught him kissing a chorus girl)

"An excuse is worse and more terrible than a lie . . ."

— Alexander Pope

It's been said that old habits die hard, implying that it's next to impossible to change long-standing thought patterns. Yet the book you hold in your hands was created out of a belief that entrenched ways of thinking and acting can indeed be eradicated. Furthermore, the most effective means for eliminating habitual thoughts is to go to work on the very system that created, and continues to support, these thinking habits. This system is made up of a long list of explanations and defenses that can be summed up in one word: *excuses*. Hence, the title of this book is really a statement to yourself, as well as to that system of explanations you've created. It is my intention that *all* excuses be . . . gone!

Can I make dramatic changes in the way I live? Is it possible to change self-defeating thoughts and behaviors that have been my constant companions for as long as I can remember? Can I really do a U-turn and deprogram myself when I've never known any other way to think and act? I've been depressed [or *stubborn, overweight, scared, clumsy, unlucky,* or any other descriptor you choose to insert here] *my entire life. Is it even feasible or practical for me to contemplate removing these old and familiar ways of being and open myself up to a brand-new me?*

This book is my answer to those questions. Yes, there *is* a way available to you, right here and right now. You can relinquish any unwanted-but-long-held thoughts that have become your self-definition. *Excuses Begone!* presents a powerful and easy method for removing deeply embedded thinking habits that are preventing you from being the person you want to be.

The power of your beliefs to keep you stuck is enormous. Those deeply ingrained notions act as chains restricting you from experiencing your unique destiny. You have the capacity to loosen these chains and make them work for, rather than against, you, to the point that you can alter what you thought were scientific explanations for your human limitations and characteristics. I'm referring to things such as your genetic makeup, your DNA, or the early conditioning imposed upon you when you were an embryo, infant, and young child. Yes, you read that correctly. *Your beliefs, all of those formless energy patterns that you've adopted as your self-image, have the ability to change dramatically and give you the power to conquer unwanted traits, or what you unhappily presume to be your fate.*

The implacable sciences of genetics, medicine, psychology, and sociology may cause you to feel helpless about overcoming "proven" facts that are said to determine virtually everything about you. "I can't help the way I think . . . I've always been this way. It's my nature and it can't be changed. This is all I've ever known. After all, you take what's handed to you, and you make the best of it." All of these are the laments of those who opt to use excuses to explain their lives away. (**Note:** I will be using the word *excuses* for what many call *conditioned ways of being.*)

Every self-limiting thought that you employ to explain why you're not living life to the absolute fullest—so you're feeling purposeful, content, and fully alive—is something you can challenge and reverse, regardless of how long you've held that belief and no matter how rooted in tradition, science, or life experience it may be. Even if it seems like an insurmountable obstacle, you can overcome these thoughts, and you can begin by noticing how they've been working to hold you back. Then you can embark on a de-programming effort that allows you to live an excuse-free life, one day at a time, one miracle at a time, one new belief at a time!

The New Word on Beliefs

Have you ever wanted to change some facet of your personality, but another part of you insisted that this is impossible because your genetic programming is responsible for how you think, feel, and behave? That latter part of you believes in biologically determined unhappy genes, shy genes, fat genes, and bad-luck genes, among many others. Due to your luck of the draw, it will tell you, you have a set of misery genes, along with a sizable cache of weight-gaining genes, if those are the aspects you want to change. This part means to be helpful—but while it probably wants to protect you from the disappointment of failure, it keeps you stuck in an excuse-driven life. Using the excuse of genetic programming *not* to do anything about the personal characteristics that you dislike is popular and clearly acceptable in today's culture.

So, using the aforementioned genetic predisposition as a rationalization, living in constant or unnecessary terror might be explained as your having an overabundance of fear cells, which you're stuck with. Thus, a formidable excuse is formulated. No wonder a part of you gets indignant when you attempt to be brave, since it believes, *I can't change my biology.* A sense of powerlessness ensues when it comes to altering anything about yourself that has become so established that it feels like who you are. This is particularly true when you observe traits and characteristics that have been with you for as long as you can recall. As if to further cement the idea that you've "always been this way" into your total worldview, the limiting part of you asserts: *There's nothing that can be done about it; after all, I can't change my basic biology.*

Excuse me—thanks to the principles I share in this book, you most certainly can!

The belief that we cannot change our biology is beginning to be challenged by scientific scholars engaged in cell-biology research. It seems that humans *do* have the ability to change and even reverse some of their genetic blueprints. Openness and curiosity, along with a desire to be free from excuses, are the basic prerequisites for learning about the exciting evidence concerning genetic predisposition.

One of the pioneers of the new way of understanding DNA, Bruce Lipton, Ph.D., is a cell biologist who taught medical students before resigning to do research and lecture full-time. In a groundbreaking book called *The Biology of Belief,* Lipton writes that life is not controlled by genes—in fact, his research led him to the conclusion that they're strictly blueprints. The invisible, formless energy that constitutes the genes' environment is the architect that turns the blueprint into this mystery we call life. Listing hundreds of research results, he concludes that the old medical model depicting life's essential building blocks as physical particles is misleading; incomplete; and, in most cases, false. Treating illness more or less exclusively with drugs or surgery to facilitate a healing begs to be reexamined.

Lipton's conclusions led to his resignation from the University of Wisconsin's School of Medicine because he discovered that what he'd been teaching (the model of physical particles as the controlling force in life) was incorrect. He realized that both the human body and the universe itself are mental and spiritual in nature. There's a field of invisible energy with a total absence of physical properties that creates the particles that we call "cells," and this invisible field is the sole governing function of the body. So, since the body is not exclusively a physical machine, we can all find out how to control and impact our health.

Even more astonishing is Lipton's understanding that our personal belief systems, including our perceptions, have the capacity to trump our genetic inheritance and our cellular DNA. It's possible to influence the infinitesimally tiny particles we've come to believe are the ultimate determiners of our lives. That is, when we change the way we think, and learn new ways of perceiving, we can actually change our DNA!

In other words, you can impact and alter your genetic structure by modifying how you see yourself and your place in this glorious mystery called life. *Your perceptions have the power to change your genetic makeup—your beliefs can and do control your biology.* This may sound radical or even impossible, yet it is this awareness that will lead you to say good-bye to the excuses you've unwittingly adopted.

I encourage you to immerse yourself in *The Biology of Belief.* You'll be inspired to reset your mind to the possibility that your beliefs carry far more weight than you realized in determining what you can do, what you'll undertake, and how far you're capable of going. Let's take a look now at another piece of research that will help you realize what you're capable of achieving.

The Placebo Effect

That the mind controls the body is hardly up for dispute. You've probably heard of documented studies where sugar pills given to a control group believing that they're a remedy for, say, arthritis, turn out to be as effective as the drug being administered for the arthritis. This placebo effect apparently occurs due to a belief in the effectiveness of the pill. But consider how powerful the mind is when it goes beyond administering a sugar pill to the world of surgery:

A Baylor School of Medicine study, published in 2002 in the *New England Journal of Medicine* evaluated surgery for patients with severe, debilitating knee pain. (Moseley, et al, 2002) The lead author of the study, Dr. Bruce Moseley, "knew" that knee surgery helped his patients. "All good surgeons know there is no placebo effect in surgery." But Moseley was trying to figure out which part of the surgery was giving his patients relief. The patients in the study were divided into three groups. Moseley shaved the damaged cartilage in the knee of one group. For another group, he flushed out the knee joint, removing material thought to be causing the inflammatory effect. Both of these constitute standard treatment for arthritic knees. The third group got "fake" surgery. The patient was sedated, Moseley made three standard incisions and then talked and acted just as he would have during a real surgery—he even splashed salt water to simulate the sound of the knee-washing procedure. After 40 minutes, Moseley sewed up the incisions as if he had done the surgery. All three groups were prescribed the same postoperative care, which included an exercise program.

The results were shocking. Yes, the groups who received surgery, as expected, improved. But the placebo group improved just as much as the other two groups! Despite the fact that there are 650,000 surgeries yearly for arthritic knees, at a cost of about $5,000 each, the results were clear to Moseley: "My skill as a surgeon had no benefit on these patients. The entire benefit of surgery for osteoarthritis of the knee was the placebo effect." Television news programs graphically illustrated the stunning results. Footage showed members of the placebo group walking and playing basketball, in short doing things they reported they could not do before their "surgery." The placebo patients didn't find out for two years that they had gotten fake surgery. One member of the placebo group, Tim Perez, who had to walk with a cane before the surgery, is now able to play basketball with his grandchildren. He summed up the theme of this book when he told the Discovery Health Channel: "In this world anything is possible when you put your mind to it. I know that your mind can work miracles." (Lipton, *The Biology of Belief*)

I believe that this kind of research offers motivating evidence for making a commitment to the *Excuses Begone!* paradigm.

Another recent procedure may completely reverse an old medical model. It seems that a man's forefinger was accidentally sliced off at the top knuckle, and by altering genetic instructions, a team succeeded in regrowing a new half-inch top to his finger in four weeks. Fingers are genetically programmed to stave off infection when an injury like this occurs, so the medical team replaced his sliced-off stub with stem cells programmed to grow a finger—the subsequent new growth included the nail, cuticle, and flesh. This man's DNA was overturned by introducing newly programmed instructions.

In a variety of studies on severe depression, heart disease, rheumatoid arthritis, ulcers, and even cancer, the power of the mind to overcome these maladies trumps the conventional medical wisdom of treating the cells rather than the environment in which they reside. The new biology is clearly indicating that beliefs—some of which are conscious and most of which are subconscious (or habitual)—determine our physical and mental health, along with our level of happiness and success.

Author James Allen observed: "We do not attract that which we *want* but that which we *are*." I've contemplated this idea for a long time. Until recently, I accepted the idea that what we are is pretty much formulated by complex genetic input and strands of DNA inherited from our parents and other relatives. But I've changed my mind. My new personal philosophy is that who I am is first and foremost determined by what I believe—and that leads me to consciously focus on the fact that limitations or traits inherited from my ancestors are absolutely not the final word. For me there's now a surprise tucked into James Allen's quote: *by changing my beliefs, I change who I am.* As a result of this shift in my beliefs, I've attracted some new and wondrous features into my life, including being prompted to write this book and share its insights with you.

As you work your way through these pages, remember that *what you are is what you believe, not what you were handed genetically.*

If you stay focused on what you are as a set of beliefs, you will align with the same kinds of energy. As you read on, remind yourself that you attract what you are, not what you want; and what you are is your beliefs, not your cells. As *The Biology of Belief* establishes, your mental activity is strong enough to overcome material particles *and* the influences of early conditioning and programming that you unwittingly adopted through your formative years.

Your Lingering Early Programming

In addition to our genetic makeup, the other big excuse that most of us use to justify unhappiness, poor health, and lack of success is the family and cultural conditioning we've been programmed with. To that end, there's a fascinating area of inquiry known as *memetics,* which deals with the mind and is analogous to the relationship of genetics to the body. So as the basic unit of genetics is the gene, the basic unit of memetics is the meme (rhymes with "team"). Yet unlike an atom or an electron, the meme has no physical properties. According to Richard Brodie, in his work *Virus of the Mind,* it's "a thought, belief, or attitude in your mind that can spread to and from other people's minds."

Richard Dawkins, the Oxford biologist who coined the word *meme,* describes the process in his book *The Selfish Gene.* My understanding is that memetics originates from the word *mimic,* meaning to observe and copy behavior. This behavior is repeated and passed on to others, and on and on the mimicking process goes. The key point is this: *transferring an idea, attitude, or belief to others is done mentally.* We won't find memes by turning up the magnification on any microscope—they pass from mind to mind via hundreds of thousands of imitations. By the age of six or seven, we've all been programmed with an endless inventory of memes that act very much like a virus. They aren't necessarily good or bad; they simply spread easily throughout the population.

Once a meme is in your mind, it can and will subtly influence your behavior. This is one of the ways you acquire a huge category of excuses that keep you in a rut. For example: "My memes made me do it! I can't help it! These ideas [beliefs, attitudes] have been passed on to me from one mind to another for generations, and there's nothing I can do about the way I think. These memes have been the building blocks of my mind, and I can't deprogram myself from these viruses of the mind that just keep replicating and spreading. These ideas [memes] are so much a part of me that it's impossible to 'disinfect' myself from the results of all of these mind viruses." Every excuse you read about in this book is, in reality, a meme that was once planted in your mind.

Richard Brodie uses the word *virus* to describe what happens in the mind through mimicking and imitating. The core purpose of a virus is to make as many copies of itself as possible by penetrating wherever an opening occurs and spreading itself to as many hosts as possible. Similarly, you're a host for countless memes; they're the entrenched thoughts and behavioral characteristics of your personality. You've spent years repeating and replicating ideas that were traveling from one mind to another, spreading these ideas and beliefs to many others.

Memes die hard because they've become who you think you are; shedding them is like trying to discard one of your vital organs, and it taps your life energy. Many memes, in fact, were firmly implanted by your parents during your early family history—it will come as no surprise that they were easily transferred to you from your parents or grandparents. Since ideas get fixed in your mind by spreading from other minds, they become your reality, often for your entire life.

Personally, I find it fascinating that there are invisible little units that I allowed to be implanted in my mind, which continue to impact how I think and behave today. Moreover, I've acted on these mind viruses and have passed them on to my children . . . unwittingly, I've become a carrier.

Here are some examples that continue to crop up in my life:

I grew up with a Depression mentality. Even though I was born in 1940 at the tail end of the Great Depression, my parents and grandparents lived through hard economic times and shared a lot of their scarcity messages with me. *Don't spend recklessly; save for the future because things will only get worse; there are shortages everywhere; food is in minimal supply; don't waste anything; eat everything on your plate; you don't have enough money . . .* these ideas were invisibly passed on to me as I grew up in the Midwest in the 1940s. I mimicked or imitated these ideas and allowed myself to become an instrument of these mind viruses. They grew in me, and I spread them wherever I went, until they became fully ensconced in my mind and many of my actions.

Although I'm now in my 60s, these memes are very much alive today and are still attempting to replicate and spread. To some extent they serve a purpose, although they occasionally work overtime. My world isn't endangered by poverty, for instance, but I'm still a financially cautious person who likes to save rather than dispose of items retaining some usefulness. I respect those attitudes, and they no doubt originated in my childhood by being programmed into my habitual subconscious mind. But do I really need to retrieve used-up toothpaste tubes discarded by my children in wastepaper baskets, and strenuously squeeze out another two weeks' worth of product . . . when I've earned enough to buy the toothpaste factory?!

Here's another mind virus I've noticed lately: I must have imitated sulking when I didn't get my way as the youngest of three boys, or as a child in a series of foster homes, because I remember my adult forms of sulking (pouting and even yelling) when I was in my 30s and 40s. Recently I was alone in my office, feeling frustrated because I couldn't locate something I needed. As my frustration mounted, I became increasingly irrational: I raised my voice, loudly protested (although there was no one else there), used profanity, and stomped through the house until I was distraught and had given myself an upset stomach. This incident lasted one or two minutes, and then I finally calmed down and found the book I thought was the culprit in my private drama.

Why am I admitting to this silly scene, given my desire to be seen as a rational spiritual teacher? Because it illustrates a point

I'm making in this opening chapter. As an embryo, an infant, and a young boy, I must have seen this kind of behavior and mimicked it—the meme infected me, replicating and spreading from a relative or friend's mind to mine. And now, some 60 years later, I could have a built-in excuse for behaving irrationally enough to feel embarrassed by my infantile behavior and for making myself sick. The excuse is right there for me to use: *I've always overreacted to frustration; it's just a part of me. I don't have any control over stomping around and blaming who knows what, using mild profanity, and being immobilized because I cannot tolerate my frustration.* The possibilities are inexhaustible for excusing this behavior, but the question I must ask myself is: *Do I really want to hold on to these habitual behaviors that are ultimately capable of making me sick?*

Just like me, you have thousands of imitated thoughts and actions that were absorbed through contact with individuals in your childhood environment. When mind viruses serve you, it's a pleasure to observe them and express silent gratitude. But when they continue to plague your life, inhibiting you from achieving your desires, then you're on notice to start shedding them. The point is that these mind viruses, or memes, can work against you in myriad ways today, but you can also change them. (I hasten to add here that by becoming aware of my own inclinations to use old, no-longer-sensible-or-practical responses to my frustrations, and by being willing to do the deprogramming work on my long-held thoughts, I now notice those infantile temptations and choose a healthier way. The bonus is that I'm more effective at locating the missing items that used to perplex me!)

Thinking that you'll always be poor, unlucky, overweight, or underweight; that you'll always have an addictive personality; that you'll never attract your soul mate; that you'll continue to have angry outbursts; that you'll always lack musical, artistic, or athletic ability; or that you'll forever be shy because you've always felt that way . . . are *excuses*. And when you see them for what they are, you can eliminate them. On the other hand, if you find them to be firmly entrenched personality traits and habits of thinking that can't be challenged, you'll symbolically suck your thumb and cry when life doesn't appear to cooperate. Believe me, though, it's far more energizing and fulfilling to practice the *Excuses Begone!* paradigm. Using a new set of thinking habits will enhance your life and help you attract all that you really are. At the same time, you'll be modeling a new and better way to live for the people in your environment who are unwitting victims of the excuse virus.

You've been a memetic superstar since birth, mimicking beliefs and behaviors from other influences beyond your family and social structure. Influences from your religious training, ethnic culture, television programming and advertising, and the like have become a fixed part of your habitual mind. It isn't my purpose to examine all the ways you've acquired beliefs, since that's something only *you* can do. I'm writing this book to help you gain awareness of the excuses you use for behaving in ways that don't help you to achieve the level of health, happiness, and success you desire. I agree with the Roman Emperor Marcus Aurelius, known for his brilliance as a leader of men and a spiritually conscious being. He is reported to have said, "Our life is what our thoughts make it."

Your behaviors are supported by your thinking patterns; that is, your thoughts truly make or break your life. While some of them are operating on a conscious level and are easy to recognize, others are deeply embedded within your subconscious. However, I prefer to call this deeply programmed or almost automatic second-nature part of you, "the habitual mind."

For me, *subconscious* implies being below the level of creative awareness, a sort of mysterious entity that can't be known. Since the central theme of this book is that anything used to explain thinking and acting in the same self-sabotaging ways is an excuse, it seems to me that calling it "subconscious" is really underscoring this notion: *I can't help it, I can't talk about it, and I certainly can't change it; because it is, after all, below my conscious level, where I do all of my living.*

I personally find it hard to work with a part of myself that's not within my conscious life. Therefore, I choose to call this huge reservoir of emptiness—a reservoir that pushes us all away from our Divine dharma as well as our optimal level of health, happiness, and success—"the habitual mind." And while these types of thoughts might seem to be unreachable, I assure you that they'll come to the surface with an *Excuses Begone!* attitude.

Kissing the Big Excuses Good-bye

This opening chapter has introduced you to recent research and observations that are increasing our understanding of human nature. My purpose is to help you use this information to alter the parts of your life that are hampered by old science and old thinking. In summary, there are basically two big excuses we all utilize:

— The first one is: *I can't really help the way I am; after all, people can't change their DNA. My genetic makeup is the culprit.* The new biology says that there's an energy field surrounding, and contained within, all of your cells, and this field is influenced by your beliefs. Moreover, it is out of this field that all particles are created —it's the sole governing entity of the body. Something like 95 percent of us do *not* have genetic reasons for illness, depression, fear, or any other condition.

Here in the 21st century, science invites you to stop believing that you're a victim of your genetic makeup, because a large body of evidence demonstrates empirically that your beliefs can change your genes. I encourage you to examine this mind-bending idea at greater depth than I'm able to offer here. There's an invisible part of you that you can call intelligence, higher function, Tao, thought, belief, Spirit, God . . . you choose.

— The second big excuse is rooted in your early history and family conditioning. It impacts you in so many ways that you probably feel it's an impossible-to-be-free-of aspect of your life.

Kiss this one good-bye as well. Just because you've been infected with a tradition meme and programmed to repeat it and pass it on to future generations doesn't mean you're unable to disinfect yourself and reprogram your inner world.

These funny little non-things called memes are thoughts that you allow to become your master—and make no mistake about it, every excuse you've ever used is really a meme disguised as an explanation. Yet you can deprogram yourself from these mind viruses. A virus isn't concerned with whether it's contributing to your well-being or your ill-being because it only wants to penetrate, replicate, and spread. But you don't have to be a victim of anything that was transferred from another mind to yours. Your beliefs have made these memes seem like second nature to you. While excuses are just thoughts or beliefs, you are the decider of what you ultimately store away as your guide to life.

A short discourse from the Dhammapada gives a sense of the route individuals travel as they advance toward their own inherent perfection and self-realization. Savor this ancient wisdom and incorporate its message with the modern understanding of genetics and memetics: "All that we are is the result of what we have thought. It is founded on our thoughts. It is made up of our thoughts. If one speaks or acts with a pure thought, happiness follows one, like a shadow that never leaves."

CHAPTER 2

YOUR TWO MINDS

*"The hell to be endured hereafter, of which theology tells,
is no worse than the hell we make for ourselves in this world
by habitually fashioning our characters in the wrong way. . . .
We are spinning our own fates, good or evil . . ."*

— from *The Principles of Psychology,* by William James

Sometime ago I challenged myself to study the process of making dramatic thought transitions, using attitudes and behaviors that had been with me for a lifetime. For several years I scrutinized precisely what I did to undo old patterns in myself. This activity led me to question basic beliefs about the legitimacy of environmental and genetic authority in determining who I am and what I can change. Due to my success in modifying my thoughts and, subsequently, my actions, I developed a new paradigm for eliminating unwanted, lifelong thinking habits. At first glance, much of what I'm sharing here may seem radical and inconsistent with established psychological and sociological academic tenets. So be it. Here is what I believe—this is how I see it!

In a brilliant one-act play by Jean-Paul Sartre titled *No Exit,* the central character states emphatically: "A man is what he wills himself to be." This idea of willpower is a core theme in much of my earlier writing, and I still strongly subscribe to the belief that we all have within us an invisible force that we recognize as *will.* But I also know that there are many facets of our lives that seem to be beyond the pale of the will—for example, it often isn't enough to eliminate lifelong habits. Identifying and changing some thoughts, particularly those that have been with us for what seems like forever, requires a brand-new perceptual process.

In contrast to Sartre's observation, Ralph Waldo Emerson offers this: "Man is a stream whose source is hidden. Our being is descending into us from we know not whence." In the 1600s, Benedict de Spinoza made a similar observation about the human mind, which I read in my college days and have never forgotten: "[T]he human mind is part of the infinite intellect of God." I still apply this to myself whenever I question how or why I got myself into one of the many predicaments I've brought upon myself throughout my adult life.

The mind that Spinoza is referring to has no form or substance; is always working—even while you're sleeping—and, most significantly, is your connection to Source. Viewed in this light, it is your personal God component, always with you and always ready to serve you in fulfilling another of Spinoza's observations: "The mind's highest good is the knowledge of God." Yes, your mind is largely responsible for who and what you've become, but there's also a beingness buried within you, in a place where your thoughts originate. Emerson suggests that it's a mystery, "descending into us from we know not whence."

These two ideas about human nature combine in you to form what I call *two minds:* The one that's frequently referred to as your "conscious mind" is what I call "creative consciousness"; and the other is your "habitual mind," which, as I explained in the last chapter, is what I call the subconscious mind. Yet whether they originate in creative consciousness or the habitual mind, I believe that any thought patterns that don't enhance and expand your joyous development are *excuses.* As you'll see, this means that you have far more influence than you've probably been led to believe to rearrange and change ineffectual and harmful beliefs or ideas.

Creative Consciousness

In this paradigm, the conscious mind is more accurately described as the *creative* conscious mind. This close-to-the-surface, nonhabitual mind makes endless decisions about what you wear, what you eat, what appointments you keep, what time you go to bed, and thousands of other daily choices in your life. This invisible and "placeless place" is the part of your brain that makes and cancels plans, adds new ones, and thinks continuously. This creative consciousness is always there, to the point that even when you want to shut it down, it can be extremely difficult to do so . . . the thoughts just keep coming. What an immeasurable benefit to consider that this vast, mysterious mind is really part of the Source that creates everything, as Spinoza suggests.

So if your mind is a creator, just as God's mind is a creator of the universe, then it can perform at the absolutely highest level imaginable. The creative force asks for nothing and has no ego—it's simply an instrument of giving, providing and offering at all times with no consideration for itself. Put another way, the highest calling of your conscious creative mind is to be the human equivalent of God's mind. Yet you'll probably agree that most of your thoughts focus on the relatively tiny universe of your human self!

Rest assured that you can choose to learn how to shift your everyday thoughts away from *What am I doing? What can I get?* and *How quickly can I get it?* to Spinoza's concept of discovering the highest-functioning, all-knowing part of yourself. This may sound like a tall order, but I guarantee that reprogramming your creative conscious mind is really a simple matter. The endless thoughts of *me, me, me* are close to the surface and highly susceptible to change. (You'll have the opportunity to practice this when you study the paradigm for eliminating excuses in the third part of this book.)

The creative conscious mind can do almost anything you instruct it to do: It can change thoughts at your bidding, practice affirmations you create, wander in blissful meditation at your invitation, and learn almost any new skill at your insistence. It can think of everything you direct it to. Through discipline, effort, and continual practice, it can also accomplish almost anything you focus your thoughts on.

The problem with creative consciousness is that its constant shifts and changes can overwhelm/flood you. It's often referred to as "the monkey mind" because it keeps flitting about almost continuously, first having one thought, then another, and then still another. Most of this close-to-the-surface mental activity is the ego's attempt to dance to the beat of rhythms and influences that are outside of you, which are probably unwanted and unnecessary, and running your life without your permission. Your creative consciousness has developed a weak connection that's full of static, so its signals from a part of the infinite intellect of God are silenced by an ego-based accompaniment that broadcasts: *What's in it for me? How do I look? How much money can I make? How can I get ahead? Whom do I have to please? Why are there so many demands on me?* On and on these thoughts come, then go, then come right back.

There's statistical evidence that the conscious mind occupies approximately 5 percent of the total workings of the brain, leaving 95 percent to the realm of the subconscious. Percentages interest me less than the ability to sense your mind as not some amorphous component of your being that's constantly changing from one ego-based thought to another, but rather as evidence of your nature, or your connection to the infinite intellect of creation. This style of magnificent respect alerts you to your ability to access the highest function of your mind.

The Habitual (Subconscious) Mind

According to Tor Nørretranders, the author of *The User Illusion,* the subconscious mind has been calculated to process millions of environmental stimuli per second versus only a few dozen environmental stimuli per second that the conscious mind can process. Conventional psychological wisdom says that much of what you believe about yourself, along with almost all of your daily actions, is programmed into your subconscious or habitual mind. You spend a great deal of your time operating on automatic pilot, so to speak. In fact, you could visualize your two minds as co-pilots: the conscious mind is aware of its thoughts but is a minor player, like a real pilot in training; while the subconscious takes care of virtually everything you need to think, say, or do.

I take exception to this assertion that the habitual mind runs the show, doing everything that the creative mind isn't paying attention to. According to this view, the habitual mind is like a computer running a downloaded program that will play throughout your life—it's been permanently programmed from the moment of conception, and it's next to impossible to get new software to rewrite existing programs. I simply cannot agree that a part of your mind was nourished by ideas, images, and input that continue to be necessary for your sustainability today. It's my contention that this is a false belief that's easily revealed as an excuse. I don't believe that anyone has to live with the belief that they have programming in their subconscious mind that can't be rewritten. I'll explain my perspective on this issue.

If you're the way you are because of something that's subconscious—that is, below your level of waking consciousness—then it's clearly something you can do nothing about. You can't even talk about it, since it's beyond your conscious mind. For the same reason, you can't understand it; you can't challenge it; and, most egregiously, you can't change or fix it. How can you fix something that's totally inaccessible? It would be like attempting to repair a broken watch that was sealed away in a vault: obviously, you'd need the combination to enter into that previously inaccessible space.

If something is subconscious and thus automatic, it's believed that you don't have a choice in the matter. And to me, that's the most regrettable thing about this subconscious model: believing that you don't have a choice. The truth, as I see it, is that everything you think, say, and do is a choice—and you don't need to think, speak, or act as you've done for your entire life. When you abandon making choices, you enter the vast world of excuses.

Right now, while reading this book, decide to begin *choosing* instead of *excusing*. You can instantly decide to reprogram and direct your life toward the level of happiness, success, and health that you prefer.

I've had a downloaded pattern since childhood, and it concerns my stroke in my daily swim. Some people who have observed me making my way through the ocean have said that I swim as though I've *had* a stroke. I never paid much attention to what others said until I discovered that the way I kicked my feet (using only my right leg, while my left leg stayed motionless) was putting undue pressure on my back and throwing me out of alignment as I practiced yoga and simply got older.

When I was advised to change the way I swam by kicking both legs simultaneously, my first reaction was to think, *I can't change my swimming style—I've been doing it this way for almost 60 years! I even swam competitively with this "Dyer stroke." This is something I've downloaded into me from thousands of hours of swimming and is a subconscious habit.* Yet after putting to the test the ideas I'm writing about in this book, I was able to rather easily adopt a brand-new swimming stroke, even though I was 65 years of age at the time.

Just like my being able to rather quickly change a 60-year-old habit, you can access the program you're operating with by examining your thoughts. Your habitual mind takes over when you choose to ignore your conscious beliefs, and you just continue to act in ways you've been programmed to. But you *can* shift to your creative mind and explore your options. You don't have to buy the old argument that a part of you is inaccessible, unreachable, or buried so deep down inside that undoing early programming is impossible. You'll never successfully reprogram your computer, or your mind, by telling it to stop spewing out the same garbage. You're stuck until you change to a new operating system or download some new files . . . but first you have to know that this is an option.

Think of the many ways in which you identify yourself, particularly in the gray area of deeply entrenched thoughts. Identify the programs in your habitual mind that are so outdated that they're hampering your system. Those attitudes, beliefs, and thoughts that don't serve you are excuses, ultimately destined to be sent to the trash bin.

Mark Twain had this wonderful observation about how we change old, unwanted ways of thinking and behaving: "Habit is habit, and not to be flung out of the window by any man, but coaxed downstairs a step at a time." My objective is to help you coax down the stairs those ways of thinking that keep you from living your life at the optimal level. Should this seem daunting, know that it doesn't have to be a lengthy, winding staircase that takes years to traverse. Or, to use the computer metaphor, your internal system is as capable of change as contemporary operating systems are. Freedom from long-established habits, whether they originated genetically or memetically, is attainable with the *Excuses Begone!* paradigm presented in Part III.

Reaching into the part of your mind that works on automatic pilot as a result of early programming and conditioning isn't nearly as troublesome as allowing it to continue to run your life. It's actually quite uncomplicated and won't take a great deal of time to shift from old habits to new choices. You are a part of the same intelligence that creates worlds; in fact, your mind *is* that intelligence. Knowing this, how could you consider a part of you to be unreachable or unprogrammable? *No* part of you is unreachable, no matter how automatic or habitual it may have become.

Certain aspects of your life may seem to be governed by a force that you're unaware of, and you can feel that there's no possibility of choice and that you're imprisoned by your excuse inventory: *I can't really help it; it's just my nature; I've always been this way.* Talk about futility! However, anytime you choose, you can access your habitual mind and begin to reprogram it, changing patterns that may have been useful once but no longer work for you.

See Yourself Through a New Lens

The quote at the beginning of this chapter was written almost 120 years ago by the father of modern psychology, William James, who urges us to be aware of the danger of living as if there are no choices. I am personally convinced that everyone has a capacity for greatness that transcends anything they've been taught to believe, that every being who's ever existed is in fact a portion of the all-creating power of intention. Since we're all pieces of the infinite creative Source, we should continually be telling ourselves, "I came from God, and since I must be like what I came from, I am a piece of the Divine." Trying to imagine the all-creating spiritual force coming up with excuses for anything is impossible, because it is creating from its own consciousness.

Now put *yourself* in this picture. While your mind is part of the unlimited Source, it becomes limited when you believe it to be *fallible, weak, impotent,* or any other adjective that misidentifies with creative energy. When you edge God out in this manner, you invite ego—which is known as the "false self" by spiritual teachers of all persuasions—in.

I invite you to try on a new lens that lets you access your false self with its ton of excuses (many of which I've detailed in the following chapter) and its belief in limitations. As it edges God out, your false self forces you to part with ideas that prove you're a spiritual being having a temporary human experience. Ego gives you a rationale for creating the rationalizations and justifications that eventually go on to direct your life. They become so embedded in what social scientists call the subconscious that your habitual mind turns into an excuse machine.

Allow yourself to look through your new lens by acquiring a set of beliefs that includes your spiritual or God-realized nature. It may feel a little unfamiliar, or even mysterious, at first, but be willing to allow your senses to adjust to this new way of seeing. Transcend the idea that your genetic makeup is static. With your new ability to perceive ego, you'll become a wizard who easily dethrones the dictator of your false self, bypassing early conditioning imposed by people in your environment who have edged God out.

As you get comfortable with this new way of seeing yourself, ask yourself the following question: *If no one told me who I was, who would I be?* Quietly meditate on this by spending some time in the spaciousness of *not knowing.* Imagine that your subconscious mind is nonexistent and there is no storage receptacle for excuses during your life. There's just an open and inviting clear space inside of you—a tabula rasa, or blank slate, with a magical surface that nothing adheres to. You might imagine that your everyday conscious mind simply doesn't absorb the opinions of the folks you grew up with. In this little fantasy, there's never been anyone telling you who you are. So who are you?

When I did this exercise, I found that my answer to the above question was quite simply: *I would be anything that I, and only I, decided to be in this moment and all future moments.* As the song goes, "I've gotta be me," and that means jettisoning all of the excuses I've accumulated. My habitual life wouldn't be based upon anyone's early programming, since there wouldn't be anyone who ever told me who I am. Or, as the Tao teaches:

> *Look to nature for your sustenance.*
> *Look to the great mysterious Tao [God] that*
> *does nothing and leaves nothing undone.*
> *Observe how the entire universe and all of*
> *these beautiful Tao-centered creatures work.*[1]

Tao-centered creatures allow. They trust. They live here in the present moment and, most assuredly, they have no need for any excuses.

Applying Your Fresh Perspective to Common Excuse Categories

Now I'd like to show you how you can take the fresh perspective you've gained by looking through your new lens. The excuse categories of genetics, memetics, and consciousness are about to be shown the door.

Your New Outlook on Genetic Programming

I'm sure you're familiar with some variation of this popular excuse: "I can't help it; it runs in my family." New biology, however, has proven that beliefs can override DNA, so move what you thought was a fact to the "excuse file" by altering how you view its authenticity. You can change what you perceive as immutable and beyond your reach by eliminating excuses such as the ones in the genetic excuse category.

As Gregg Braden writes in his astonishing book *The Spontaneous Healing of Belief:*

> Paradigm-shattering experiments published in leading-edge, peer-reviewed journals reveal that we're bathed in a field of intelligent energy that fills what used to be thought of as empty space. Additional discoveries show beyond any reasonable doubt that this field responds to us—*it rearranges itself*—in the presence of our heart-based feelings and beliefs. And this is the revolution that changes everything.

Here are two exercises to practice applying these ideas to your genetic program:

1. Be open to the scientifically verified idea that your beliefs have the power to rearrange and change the material world. Start by making this particularly pertinent for you in your physical and personal destiny by contemplating that more things of this nature are possible than you've previously experienced. Allow these new

thoughts about your biology to gently enter your belief system. Encourage yourself to consider your beliefs as things that affect you, perhaps even more than physical particles do. If it suits you, you may even see beliefs as nonparticles in the nonmaterial or spiritual world.

2. Create an affirmation that attests to this new no-excuses philosophy for genetics. Something from the following list would work fine, but feel free to come up with your own:

- *I can change my body's infirmities by shifting my beliefs.*

- *I have the power to undo old thoughts about my genetic destiny.*

- *If I stay with them and live from my heart, my beliefs can inspire new talents if I so desire.*

- *I can heal anything by healing my beliefs first.*

- *I intend to keep my beliefs uppermost, and I refuse to blame anything in the material world for any deficiencies in my life.*

Your New Outlook on Memetic Programming

Again, this is an excuse category that you've probably depended on to justify why life isn't what you really want it to be. These are the big mind-virus excuses: *My family made me the way I am, and I can't change it. My early childhood experience and all of the unfair criticism I received explain why I have low self-esteem. I'm stuck in this place because I've been infected by a multitude of mind viruses and environmental facts that have left me shortchanged when it comes to fulfilling a higher destiny. How can I change what I've imitated and mimicked for so many years? I've been infected by mind viruses, and it's impossible to change.*

What follows are two exercises to practice applying to your memetic program:

1. Affirm: *I believe that I am perfectly capable of overcoming any early conditioning I have adopted as a part of my personality and my current life experience.* Know that research is demonstrating that the power of thought is aligned with the universal mind, which many call "the Tao" or "God." Just hang on to this idea for now—it will become clearer as you progress through this course in *Excuses Begone!*

2. Assert that anything that's been programmed into you and acts like a virus is perfectly capable of being *de*programmed if you decide it's worth the effort. Remind yourself that since you're not presently a victim of beliefs that were modeled for you when you were much younger, using these as excuses is no longer your method. At this point you don't even have to know how to deprogram or disinfect yourself. All you need to believe is that you have the ability and will begin now.

Here's an affirmation that will guide you to awareness and answers: *I am much more powerful today than the old programs and mind viruses that I absorbed in my childhood.* Telling yourself this will make your inner teacher appear!

Your New Outlook on Creative Consciousness

The everyday activity of your creative consciousness also proliferates excuses. You might think that you have no control over the thoughts that just keep popping into your head, but consider this radical idea: *Your thoughts are not located in your head.* Thought is an energy system that isn't found anywhere in the physical world. The universe itself and everything in it is both mental and spiritual in nature. You create a field of energy with your thoughts, and the field creates all of the particles, or what Lao-tzu called "the world of the 10,000 things." This energy field is an important function of the body; your conscious mind is always working and connecting to this field from which everything is intended.

Apply these two exercises:

1. Quiet the mind by practicing daily meditation. As Sogyal Rinpoche wrote in *The Tibetan Book of Living and Dying:* "The gift of learning to meditate is the greatest gift you can give yourself in this life. For it is only through meditation that you can undertake the journey to discover your true nature, and so find the stability and confidence you will need to live, and die, well." Find a way to give yourself that gift and access your conscious creative mind by eliminating unnecessary, unwanted, superfluous thoughts through meditation.

2. Use positive proclamations daily that are life enhancing and align you with the loving Source of everything. Rather than allowing your thoughts to insist that something is wrong or missing, retrain your conscious creative mind with beliefs such as these: *What I desire is already here; I just haven't connected to it yet. It can't be stopped because my thoughts are aligned with the mind or intellect of God.*

Your New Outlook on Habitual Consciousness

In this category you'll find excuses such as: *I can't help the way I am because I've had so many limiting ideas programmed into me. It's my subconscious, so I can't even reach in there and examine it, let alone deprogram myself.* If you believe that your mind is below your level of conscious awareness, you've created a ready excuse to use whenever it's difficult to change your thinking. And if the self-limiting thoughts have been with you for years, it seems like a perfect excuse. So rename the subconscious mind the *habitual* mind.

Habit implies that you've made the same choices over time, and your thoughts and behaviors are simply accustomed to a certain way of being. It also suggests that there's room to make your thoughts less automatic and more aligned with the realm of choice. Later you'll read about awareness as one of the keys to bringing these thoughts into your daily experience; but for now, practice the following as you start to eliminate excuses from your habitual mind:

1. Begin noticing what you're thinking as a way to weaken your reliance on the excuse of your subconscious. Repeating these quotes can be helpful: "Every extension of knowledge arises from making conscious the unconscious" (Friedrich Nietzsche), and "The unconscious . . . is dangerous only when our conscious attitude towards it becomes hopelessly false" (from *Modern Man in Search of a Soul*, by Carl Jung). Two of the world's greatest teachers state that you can change previously unconscious thinking habits and bring them to your conscious mind. Relying upon the excuse of a subconscious mind is both false and dangerous.

Why not create your version of those quotes as well? Try something like: "I am perfectly capable of reaching into my own mind and changing anything about myself that is supported by my habitual thinking patterns, even if they seem to be automatic at this point in time." Speak your truth in a way that assists your choice to rid yourself of those excuses.

2. Make this a motto for your thoughts: *Do good things, and don't do bad things!* Bad thoughts prompt you to engage in self-limiting behaviors; good thoughts, on the other hand, support your desire and capacity to live at high levels of joy, success, and health.

Here's some advice from ancient China, attributed to a fictional character named Birdsnest:

> Long ago in China, there lived a monk who perched in a
> certain tree every day to meditate. No matter if the tree swayed

30

in fierce winds and rain, the monk settled himself comfortably, high up in the branches. Because of this, he was nicknamed "Birdsnest" by the village folk nearby.

Many of these villagers passed beneath the monk while hunting or while gathering wood in the forest, and after a time, they grew used to him. Some began to stop and talk of their concerns with Birdsnest. They liked the things he had to say, and soon Birdsnest became known for his kind and thoughtful words.

After some years, the monk's wise reputation spread throughout the province. Visitors from distant cities hiked to the remote forest for advice. Even the governor of the province decided that he too would like to visit Birdsnest to discuss matters of importance. So one spring morning, the governor set off to find him. After traveling for several days, he at last located Birdsnest's tree in the dense forest. The monk sat calmly, high in the topmost branches, enjoying the warmth and the birdsong of spring.

Looking up, the governor shouted, "Birdsnest! I am the governor of this province, and I have come a great distance to speak with you! I have a most important question!" The governor waited for a reply but heard only the pleasant sounds of leaves stirring in the breeze. The governor continued, "This is my question: tell me, Birdsnest, what is it that all the wise ones have taught? Can you tell me the most important thing the Buddha ever said?" There was a long pause—just the soft rustle of leaves again.

Finally, the monk called down from the tree: "This is your answer, Governor: Don't do bad things. Always do good things. That's what all the Buddhas taught."

But the governor thought this answer far too simple to have walked two days for! Irritated and annoyed, he stammered, "Don't do bad things; always do good things! I knew that when I was three years old, monk!"

Looking down at the governor, Birdsnest replied with a wry smile, "Yes, the three-year-old knows it, but the eighty-year-old still finds it very difficult to do!"

When it feels difficult to do good things, remember to seek the three-year-old within that Birdsnest referred to. Give yourself the gift of hearing thoughts from a time before conditioning was deeply embedded.

CHAPTER 3

YOUR EXCUSE CATALOG

*"I know of no more encouraging fact than the unquestionable
ability of man to elevate his life by a conscious endeavor."*
— from *Walden,* by Henry David Thoreau

I have an undeniable affinity for Henry David Thoreau's experience while communing with nature at Walden Pond in Massa-
chusetts. I've visited his home in Concord on many occasions,
meditated at his desk, and rested on his bed to enhance this magical connection. The quote above is so meaningful to me that it
actually influenced my writing of this book!

I've occasionally been accused of being a Pollyanna, offering
hope to the hopeless. Some see my philosophy concerning the
human ability to elevate life to higher levels of peace, love, and
joy to be naïve. Being compared to Pollyanna isn't a source of discomfort for me, however. After all, here was a little girl who arrived
in a town where the people were miserable and pessimistic, with
doom and gloom dominating the horizon. Within a short while,

the energy of Pollyanna permeated the community—her enthusiasm was infectious; and people began to feel hope, passion, and love replacing their despair and futility. So if I'm to be compared to anyone, I find it an honor to be viewed in Pollyannish terms. I think that many of Mr. Thoreau's contemporaries might have applied a similar label to him as well.

Thoreau left the corrupt world of humankind to live in the natural world, with trees, animals, and the weather as his teachers. He discovered an ecstatic awareness of a current of life coursing though the entire planet, which led to his optimism about human potential. His message is essentially this: *Realize the existence of the unknowable and ecstatic aspect of your existence. Know that this Divine element is an intrinsic part of yourself. Begin trusting your underlying nature by becoming conscious.* In other words, excuses be . . . gone!

There are four words in this chapter's opening quote that I want to highlight—*encouraging, unquestionable, elevate,* and *conscious:*

1. This book is *encouraging* you to challenge patterns and feel inspired by a newfound awareness of the life hidden beneath your excuses. Invite yourself to move out of established thought patterns, and realize that there is nothing standing in your way of living at your highest levels.

2. You have an *unquestionable* ability to eliminate excuses—they'll get up and go when they're revealed as the false beliefs that they are. There's simply no question about this!

3. You *elevate* your life by taking responsibility for who you are and what you're choosing to become. You can transcend the ordinary, mundane, and average with thoughts of greater joy and meaning; you can decide to elevate your life, rather than have it stagnate or deteriorate with excuses. Go beyond where you presently are.

4. You can bring your desires to consciousness by disconnecting the power from your subconscious so that it can't continue to run your life. Your subconscious (habitual) mind is accessible, so unearth the excuses buried deep within you. Become *conscious!*

Be *encouraged* by the *unquestionable* ability you have to *elevate* your life by a *conscious* endeavor. Remember these four words as you review the following list of some of the most common excuses that you'd probably like to free yourself from.

A Catalog of Some Common Excuses

In my role as a counselor, teacher, and parent, I've heard many reasons that people use to explain an unhappy existence . . . and almost all of them inevitably fall into one huge category, which I call "excuses." The rest of the chapter will introduce you to 18 of the most commonly used ones, along with a brief commentary about each of them. This will give you a primer before you go on to learn the *Excuses Begone!* method that's detailed in the rest of the book.

Here they are, in no particular order:

1. It Will Be Difficult

While this may seem like a supportable reason, it's clearly an excuse designed to discourage you. If you're honest with yourself about the difficulty you're experiencing with addiction, obesity, depression, shyness, low self-esteem, loneliness, or any other life aspect, you'll recognize the *useless suffering* you're hanging on to. If it's going to be difficult anyway, why not opt for some use*ful* suffering? Still, the fact is that you have absolutely no incontrovertible evidence that what you'd like to change is actually going to be challenging. It's just as likely to be easy for you to change your thinking as it is to be hard.

Decades ago when I decided to give up smoking, for example, I used *Excuses Begone!* beliefs. It was encouraging for me to realize how much more difficult it was to smoke than not to smoke. The smoker part of me always had to have a pack of cigarettes and an ashtray within easy reach, carry matches or lighters, dispose of ashes, deal with smelly fingers and stained teeth, earn money to pay for this disgusting habit, be careful exhaling noxious fumes, cough up nicotine residue from my lungs, buy lighter fluid and flints, and on and on. The truth was that continuing to smoke was the real difficulty, and changing my habit involved one simple thing: not smoking.

This is true for virtually all of your habits. The belief that they're going to be hard to change is only a belief! Making something difficult in your mind before you even undertake the effort is an excuse. *Nothing in the world is difficult for those who set their mind to it,* as an ancient Taoist master concluded.

2. It's Going to Be Risky

Again, this may seem like a good reason, but if you convince yourself that something involves more risk than you're capable of assuming or have the strength for, this is a poor excuse for not taking action. What is unquestionable here is your ability to choose your belief about the drawbacks of this endeavor.

Over the years, countless people have thanked me for taking so many risks in speaking out about what I believe so fervently. I'm always taken aback by such expressions of gratitude—I've never assumed that I was being courageous by speaking my mind. Even if my opinions and statements were certain to be perceived as offensive by large numbers of people, the idea that being myself and also being willing to express my own truth involved taking a chance never occurred to me.

I don't believe you can ever be 100 percent certain that something will be risk free. Holding back in silence out of fear of retribution or criticism could actually be the more hazardous behavior.

Speaking from the heart doesn't always mean critical fallout; after all, about 99 percent of the time, the feedback I receive is positive and heartwarming.

The fear involved in anticipating a risk simply serves to keep you from taking action. When you convince yourself that it's your job to avoid taking chances, you can continue your familiar habits. If you're accustomed to playing it safe by attempting to please everyone you encounter, then you're a victim of your own excuse making.

The point is that if you fear the opinions of others—or if you fear failure or success—then anything that you think or do will involve some risk. But if you're willing to live from *your* convictions and fulfill *your* destiny, then what others perceive as taking chances are simply the ways you choose to elevate your life. Even if you do believe that changing the way you think will involve risks, so what? The peace that you feel because you ignored the worry of a risk is far greater than staying stuck in a belief that is really only an excuse.

As writer Logan Pearsall Smith once noted: "What is more mortifying than to feel that you have missed the plum for want of courage to shake the tree?"

3. It Will Take a Long Time

Is this a valid reason, or an excuse not to proceed? If you wish to elevate your life, it really doesn't matter how long it takes, does it? And this is particularly true when you're conscious that *you live your life, every single bit of it, in the present moment and only in the present moment.* All you ever get is now. Every thought occurs in the present moment, and every change has a defining moment. Often it takes something or someone outside of you to help you realize that.

An entertaining psychiatrist named Dr. Murray Banks does just that with the following little exchange between himself and a woman who has decided not to return to school because she'd be too old when she finished.

"How old would you be in five years if you got that degree by starting now?" he asks her.

"Forty-nine," she replies.

"And how old will you be in five years if you don't go back to school?"

"Forty-nine," she answers, seemingly confused . . . but with the look of one who's become conscious of the excuses she created for not elevating her life.

However long it took you to create any self-defeating habit, you did it all one day, one moment at a time. There's absolutely no proof that anything will take a long time, since even the idea of "a long time" is an illusion—there is only now. Make this awareness a part of your consciousness. The Tao Te Ching reinforces this in perhaps the most famous line in that masterful work: "A journey of a thousand miles begins with a single step." Elevate or move on in your life, not by thinking big and in long time periods, but with consciousness focused on the present moment.

4. There Will Be Family Drama

After spending many years as a family therapist, I've seen how people often become stuck in their habituated modes of thinking because they fear the criticism that could result if they change. And I receive so many phone calls on my weekly radio show (on **HayHouseRadio.com**®) from individuals who insist on remaining stuck because of this excuse. When I encourage a shift in thinking, I regularly hear things like, "I'd love to try what you suggest, but it would kill my parents," or "My family would disown me if I did that! It's too big a price to pay." I've heard more than a few admit that if their spouse died, it would be an easier solution than making changes!

Now let me be very clear here: *I believe in family.* I have eight beautiful children, a mother in her 90s whom I adore, and two brothers whom I love dearly; and I treasure my immediate and extended families.

However—and this is a crucial point—living a life of your own choosing involves the unquestionable willingness to endure the slings and arrows that could come your way when you respond to your inner knowing rather than to the opinions of your family. Samuel Butler was probably feeling something similar when, toward the end of his life in 1902, he wrote: "I believe more unhappiness comes from this source than from any other—I mean the attempt to prolong family connection unduly, and to make people hang together artificially who would never naturally do so."

You don't belong to your immediate family; you're a member of the *human* family. You don't own your children, nor are you a possession of your parents. You're not obliged to fulfill the wishes or a destiny dictated by kin. It's important to consciously know that you're here to create your music, and that you don't have to die with your music still in you. Granted, this can trigger some family drama, but then again, that might just be your excuse for not following your own path. It's been my experience that I earn far more respect than reproach from my family whenever I encourage myself to live the life I want.

To that end, these types of excuses need to disappear: "I can't disappoint my grandparents or my parents. Why should I be the only one rebelling and wanting to move out of town? Or take up a new occupation? Or marry outside of our faith [or whatever else may incur disapproval and censure from relatives]?" These are thoughts or memes based on fears that were originally internalized in childhood, when they seemed the only way to secure a place in your "tribe." Yet what were reasons to the child you were then need to be recognized as excuses by the adult you are today. Don't let fear of family dramas keep you from changing outmoded, unnecessary, and unwanted thought patterns.

5. I Don't Deserve It

In *Revolution from Within: A Book of Self-Esteem,* Gloria Steinem writes that "self-esteem isn't everything; it's just that there's nothing without it." I believe that lack of self-esteem is the basis for the "I don't deserve it" excuse. I hear it in sentences such as these: "Nothing seems to work for me," "I try, but nothing ever comes my way . . . I must not be worthy of it," and "Other people can get ahead, but I guess I'm not good enough to succeed."

These excuses are based on a belief in the validity of your unworthiness. It's as if a part of you wants to protect you from (what's assumed to be) the unbearable pain of feeling that *maybe they're right, and I don't deserve it.* If you ask that part of you why it's doing this, it will have good reasons. But those reasons are, in effect, lies, and functioning by their edict means that you're *living* a lie. You don't earn worthiness—you're equally as deserving of all that this glorious world offers as anyone else is.

Believing that you're not good enough to have unlimited happiness, success, and health is a colossal fabrication that bears no resemblance to the truth of your life today. It keeps you discouraged, with a well-intentioned excuse to protect you from taking action. But it isn't *protecting* you; it's *preventing* you from becoming conscious of your unquestionable worthiness. In the presence of now, this excuse has no place in your life.

6. It's Not My Nature

The sentences cropping up in this category sound something like this: "I've always been this way; I can't help it," "I was born with these personality traits," "I've never known any other way to think," and "Yep, it's my nature, so I'll have to accept it." Earlier in this book, I explained my understanding of new research demonstrating that your genetic and memetic heredities are capable of being altered. If you're willing to consciously endeavor to change the beliefs that support what you call your nature, you'll discover that the "it's not my nature" excuse is gone.

I firmly believe that your intrinsic self is well equipped to help you fulfill your unique destiny. Just because you have no recollection of ever having been other than you are today, this isn't proof that your nature is unchangeable. To once again quote Henry David Thoreau: "It is surprising how much room there is in nature, if a man will follow his proper path." I take this to mean that nature itself will shift to accommodate you when you begin to know your unquestionable ability to elevate your life. Incorporate Thoreau's advice and begin to follow your own path. Recognize excuse logic that sounds like this: "I've always been this way; it's just who I am. I'd like to change, but how can I change my own nature? It's all I've ever known, so I guess I'll just have to stay the way I am."

Can you see how this kind of logic keeps you stuck in a life-long thinking habit? The very fact that you've been a certain way throughout your life is a perfect reason for encouraging yourself with thoughts such as: *I'm fed up with being frightened, shy, poor, unhappy, used by others, condescending, fat, or out of shape. It's all I've ever known, and it stems from the way I think and the beliefs I've come to accept as defining my nature. If this is my nature, then I'm going to change it, beginning right now.* Now these are notions that the philosopher Bertrand Russell could get behind. He wrote: "If human nature were unchangeable, as ignorant people still suppose it to be, the situation would indeed be hopeless . . . what passes as 'human nature' is at most one-tenth nature, the other nine-tenths being nurture."

So whatever you believe is your nature, allow it to be nurtured the way you'd like it to be, starting with *Excuses Begone!* Nine-tenths of your nature has been learned and adopted as a habit, and you can coax those old habits down the stairs, one step at a time.

7. I Can't Afford It

It's a rare day when I don't hear some variation of this excuse, including: "I didn't go to college because it was too expensive," "I haven't been able to travel because I never had the funds," and "I couldn't go into the business I wanted because I had to stay where I was and earn money to pay the bills." I call this belief lame and a cop-out, yet there seems to be almost universal agreement for its existence.

You originated in a world of abundance, which you unquestionably have the ability to access. Whenever you discourage yourself with thoughts that your financial situation is preventing anything from appearing, that's an excuse. If you instead decide to bring abundance awareness into your consciousness, you'll shift your thoughts from *I can't afford it* to *Whatever I need in the form of assistance to guide me in the direction of my life is not only available, but is on its way.* You'll then consciously watch for the necessary funding to show up, but you'll also be reminding yourself to believe that you have the ability to use abundance to elevate your life.

Encourage yourself by realizing that you have the capacity to create a space within you that's filled with peace and joy, an inner island of contentment that has nothing to do with money. Practice gratitude for the essentials of life, which are yours to enjoy virtually free of charge. These include air, water, fire, the sun, and the moon; the very ground you walk on; the continuous beating of your heart; the inhaling and exhaling of your lungs; your food digesting; your eyes and ears; and so on. Be utterly grateful for all that you have naturally, which is beyond the scope of what's "affordable." As that endeavor strengthens, assess what you'd truly like to do, where you'd like to live, and what creature comforts you desire.

When I made the decision to attend college after spending four years in the military, for instance, I knew in my heart that money wasn't going to be the thing that prevented me from reaching my goals. I understood the costs involved, and I didn't act on my fear of shortage or what I couldn't afford—I acted on my internal knowing that I indeed was going to attend a university. This knowing prompted me to investigate financial assistance from the government as a veteran, open a savings account designated for tuition and books, talk with the financial-aid people at the university I was interested in, and make alternative plans to attend community college, if plan A were not to materialize. I had a certainty inside of me that the "I can't afford it" reasoning is an excuse that many people who aren't considered wealthy employ as a means for exonerating themselves when they need a rationalization for why they're stuck where they are in life.

Oscar Wilde made this wry observation in 1891: "There is only one class in the community that thinks more about money than the rich, and that is the poor. The poor can think of nothing else." I'd add that such thinking includes lamenting the fact that they'll *never* have money. I advise tossing out this meme, and instead rewiring thoughts to connect with what's *intended* to manifest, regardless of your current financial status.

Whatever you feel is your *dharma,* and no matter how hard that calling seems to be pulling you, if you maintain the belief that you can't manage to pull it off, I can assure you that you're right. To paraphrase Henry Ford, whether you believe you can afford to do a thing or not, you're right.

8. No One Will Help Me

This excuse really saddens me because there's no truth in it whatsoever. The fact is that the world is filled with people who would jump at the chance to help you with whatever you'd like to create. But if you hold on to a false notion that no one will be there to help you, your experiences will match that belief.

If you've spent way too much of your life overweight, seriously addicted, lost in poverty, or what have you, then you need to realize that the ball is in *your* court—no more excuses! Once that belief begins changing, you'll see help arriving, but the initial movement is completely in your thoughts. It begins with this new belief: *I can access help.*

Begin encouraging yourself with affirmations that support and elevate your beliefs, such as: *I have the capacity to create by myself if necessary, I know the right people to help me are here at the right time,* and *The world is full of people who would love to assist me.* These will help to align you with the source of energy that's always available to your intuitive self. Elevate your confidence further with this journal entry made in November 1843 by Ralph Waldo Emerson: "[I]f I have lost confidence in myself I have the Universe against me." *You* are the universe; you originated from the invisible world of Spirit. When you doubt yourself, you doubt the universal intelligence that you are, and it seems there's no one to help you.

As an example from my own life, I repeat this thought from *A Course in Miracles* when I'm about to give a speech: "If you knew who walked beside you at all times on this path that you have chosen, you could never experience fear or doubt again." As I approach the microphone/podium, I remember that I'm an instrument for the words and ideas. My confidence trusts the wisdom that created me. In other words, I know that I am never alone. *No one will help me* becomes an invalid excuse.

I affirm that all that is needed or required will be there, and I consciously encourage myself with this unquestionable certainty. And help seems to come from all directions: The money I need somehow shows up, the right people emerge, and circumstances occur that are unexpectedly helpful—almost as if some synchronistic force steps in and bewilders me with the beauty of it all! I'm encouraged by my unquestionable power to elevate myself in any situation.

9. It Has Never Happened Before

"Be not the slave of your own past," my literary soul mate, Ralph Waldo Emerson, wrote in his journal. Just because you've "always" been a particular way, this isn't a rational explanation for your present state of affairs. In fact, it's an excuse attempting to explain away what you feel are shortcomings.

The past is a trail you leave behind, much like the wake of a speedboat. That is, it's a vanishing trail temporarily showing you where you were. The wake of a boat doesn't affect its course—obviously it can't, since it's only appears *behind* the boat. So consider this image when you exclaim that your past is the reason you aren't moving forward.

The logic of *It's never happened before* or its equally debilitating corollary, *It's always been that way for me*, stems from these beliefs: *My past is over, and what's over can't be changed. What happened before will happen again, so I'm being guided today by what can't be changed; therefore, it's impossible for me to change. It's over for me. What I want has never happened before, and that means it will never, ever happen.* This is what happens when you live in the trail you've left behind: convinced that your past is the reason why you can't change, you hang on to it to excuse yourself from thinking differently.

Consciously choose a new set of affirmations that encourage you to believe in your ability to elevate your life above past levels. Try: *I can accomplish anything I put my mind to here in the present moment. My past has no bearing on what I can and will create. If it has never happened before, that is all the more reason for me to make it happen now. I will cease being a slave to my past.* Inventory the mental excuses you have for avoiding risk, failure, criticism, ridicule, or the negative opinions of others. See how you're creating them as the formation of your current excuse memes. Yes, I said memes—those ideas placed in your head from mimicking the ideas of others until they've become a set of mind viruses. When they're put to the seven-part *Excuses Begone!* paradigm in Part III of this book, they'll simply crumble right before your eyes because they have no substance.

I doubt this point could be better summarized than in the last lines of Carl Sandburg's poem "Prairie":

> *I tell you the past is a bucket of ashes.*
> *I tell you yesterday is a wind gone down,*
> *a sun dropped in the west.*
> *I tell you there is nothing in the world*
> *only an ocean of tomorrows,*
> *a sky of tomorrows.*

Give up hanging on to that bucket of ashes.

Recently I spent an afternoon swimming with the dolphins in the Mexican Riviera. I'd never done such a thing in all of my 68 years. But rather than telling myself that I couldn't undertake such an outing because *it's never happened before,* I reversed the logic and instead thought, *Since I've never done this before, I want to add this to my repertoire and have this unique experience right now.* And it was sensational!

Adopt this kind of thinking regarding everything you've "never done" before. Open up to vistas that bring you to a new way of being where you create wealth, health, and happiness in the present moment.

10. I'm Not Strong Enough

The "I'm not strong enough" excuse unquestionably keeps you locked into a habituated way of thinking. Years spent believing in your weakness actually strengthens the belief that you aren't an emotionally, spiritually, or physically capable individual. It only takes a little bit of criticism to discourage you and activate this belief: *I'm not a strong person, so I'll resort to my true self, who is weak.* The idea that you aren't tough enough to hold a certain job, stand up to a bully or victimizer, take care of yourself, face life alone, or travel by yourself are all mind viruses that are ready excuses when life gets tough. This is true on a collective level as well.

I spent a couple of years teaching American history, with a special interest in colonial America. I was always intrigued by how the United States broke free from the small island on the other side of the ocean that had ruled it with an iron fist for so many years. The message that the British had always sent was: "We are strong, and you, fledgling wannabes, are weak." The result was a kind of servitude that had kept the colonists in excuse mode but was ultimately brought to a halt once and for all.

The transformation required a paradigm shift, which ultimately resulted in new thinking habits. It began with that great assortment of Founding Fathers from north to south, who challenged the mind virus that they were weak and the British were strong. When enough of these courageous leaders shared their beliefs about American might, the new meme began to replicate, infiltrate, and spread throughout the 13 colonies. In that vein, here's a portion of a speech delivered by Patrick Henry before the Second Revolutionary Convention of Virginia in 1775: "[W]e are not weak if we make a proper use of those means which the God of nature has placed in our power. . . . The battle, sir, is not to the strong alone; it is to the vigilant, the active, the brave."

Shift out of the mental belief that you're too weak. Become vigilant and active, and demonstrate a new kind of bravery. Affirm that you're breaking free of thinking habits that have convinced you you're not a strong person. Here are some affirmations: *I shall never see myself as lacking in strength again. What you think of me is none of my business. My strength is my connection to Source; it does not know weakness.*

Become conscious of the fact that seeing this belief as an excuse illuminates its weakness, but it also strengthens your ability to encourage yourself. You possess all the fortitude of character, mind, and body to live at the highest levels of happiness, health, and prosperity. Let these words of Mohandas K. Gandhi inspire you: "Strength does not come from physical capacity. It comes from an indomitable will."

11. I'm Not Smart Enough

Your vast intelligence isn't measurable by an IQ test, nor is it susceptible to the analysis of school transcripts. Your ideas or beliefs about what you'd like to be, accomplish, or attract are evidence of your genius. If you're capable of conceiving it, then that act of visual conception, combined with your passion for manifesting your idea into reality, is all you need to activate your genius. If you think that it's impossible to categorize yourself as a genius, I emphatically ask: *Why not?* You originated in the same infinite field of intention as everyone else who's ever lived. Your mind is a component of the mind of God or the universal Tao, so how could it be other than the brilliance of the Creator? Were you not created out of this vast sea of invisible intelligence? Are your ideas somehow inferior, or incapable of being transformed into this material world? Even as a part of you hangs on to the "I'm not smart enough" excuse, another part recognizes this truth.

When you state, "I've never been smart enough," you're really saying, "I've bought into a definition of intelligence that's measured by what family members or educators provided me with earlier in life." You can give yourself encouraging input instead of the discouraging messages from your past by knowing that intelligence can never be measured, nor can it in any way be limited. So if you're willing to put your passion and perseverance into your ideas, you'll meet the genius part of you. Even if you subscribe to the idea that this excuse is warranted because your brain is somehow not up to par, consider the conclusions that Sharon Begley offers in her book *Train Your Mind, Change Your Brain*. Here's what she says about the power of the brain to change, not through prescription drugs, but through the will: "The conscious act of thinking about one's thoughts in a different way changes the very brain circuits that do that thinking . . ." and "The ability of thought and attention to physically alter the brain echoes one of Buddhism's more remarkable hypotheses: that will is a real, physical force that can change the brain."

So even if you want to hang on to the excuse that your brain is chemically deficient, you have within you the power to change its material makeup—you can rearrange your old thinking system so that it conforms with the genius model. Why not think that the ideas in your head are by-products of your genius instead of a limited intelligence? Let what Oscar Wilde is said to have remarked to a New York City customs official encourage you. When asked if he had anything to declare, he responded, "I have nothing to declare but my genius," and in many ways, he was absolutely correct.

When you trust in yourself, you trust in the very wisdom that created you. Make a conscious effort not to second-guess that originating wisdom. Like Oscar Wilde, have only your genius to declare. Trust your elevated thoughts, especially those that stir up passion, and then act on them as if they were unquestionable.

12. I'm Too Old (or Not Old Enough)

The age of your body can seem to be quite an obstacle on the road to changing long-held thinking habits, particularly since you received an extensive list of memes concerning age very early on. Depending on where you grew up, you heard statements such as: "You can't ride your bicycle until you're seven," "You can't sleep over until you're ten," "You can't drive a car until you're 16," and "You can't have sex until you're married." Then at some point you discovered that you went from being not old enough to being too old! Then you started to hear: "You can't get a new job after age 35," "You can't change occupations because you're past your prime," "You can't fall in love again at your age," "It's too late to write the book or compose the symphony you've always dreamed about," and, of course, "You can't teach an old dog new tricks." And all of these memes became your reality.

The age excuse comes from an inclination to identify yourself with the number of trips you've made around the sun rather than from the unlimited side of you that lives independent of the age of your body. Part of you has an ageless mind and is quite oblivious to the physical aging process—and it's available to you if you'll just encourage it with conscious invitations to participate in your life.

As a young child, you had daydreams about what you might invent, draw, write, or design. Mind viruses came your way routinely, which made age your reality. "Wait until you're bigger to do those kinds of things" seemed to be a never-ending pronouncement, all too quickly turning into: "You're too old; act your age; it's too late." Somewhere between the two, your private destiny wasn't elevated to a primary position in your life.

You are the age you are—period. Yet those thoughts swirling around inside and outside of your head are ageless. They have no form. No boundaries. No beginnings. No endings. When you speak of age, you speak of your body, this finite thing that houses your invisible essence. This excuse is all about your physical self, and it is unquestionably influenced by your mind. You're the perfect age right here in this moment, and your body can be no other age than what it is. Identify yourself in what Lao-tzu calls "the subtle realm," or the invisible domain of Spirit, with thoughts like these: *I am ageless, and I can train my body to work with me in achieving anything I can conceive of in my mind. There's nothing about my age today that prohibits me from fulfilling my dreams. My mind is free, and I can train it to do my bidding rather than acquiescing to an excuse pattern.*

I've had two very persuasive callings in my life. One occurred when I knew I'd be pursuing a college education regardless of being the oldest freshman on campus. Age was of no consequence to me. In fact, the eight years I spent as a student on several college campuses to earn my three academic degrees were accomplished in part because I was so unconcerned about my age. I was living my passion, and everything else took a backseat to that vision.

My second huge calling came at the age of 65 years and one day. Compelled to detach myself from worldly possessions accumulated over many decades, I disposed of clothes, furniture, books, records, awards, photographs, and memorabilia of all description. Studying and living the Tao Te Ching, I wrote an essay on each of the 81 verses in a book titled *Change Your Thoughts—Change Your Life*. That I might be too old simply never occurred to me.

As I look back on my life, I realize that I've made many smaller decisions where I refused to consider age as a factor. At the age of 42, I decided to become a long-distance runner and ran the original Greek marathon. At the age of 17, I decided to write my first novel; and at the age of 9, I faked my age to get a paper route (10 was the "required" age). At the age of 68, I can't conceive of thinking that I'm too old to do what I love. Without that excuse, I continue to live life by activating my particular dharma or destiny. In fact, I just completed a brand-new career undertaking as an actor and a filmmaker—I encourage you to view *The Shift* and tell me if you think I was too old for such a project.

13. The Rules Won't Let Me

Perhaps the most famous of Henry David Thoreau's observations is this one from the conclusion of *Walden:* "If a man does not keep pace with his companions, perhaps it is because he hears a different drummer." Thoreau is referring to the unlikelihood of being able to always march to the same beat as everyone else. There are times in your life when you have to listen to the rhythm of rules that are beating within you, and only you, instead. But perhaps you've latched on to a belief that the rules of society are so sacrosanct that bending them would be crossing a line that you (or anyone) should never cross. The words that follow the above sentence in *Walden* are even more compelling for living an *Excuses Begone!* life: "Let him step to the music which he hears, however measured or far away." I'm not making a case for being a lawbreaker just for the sake of nonconformity—I *am* encouraging you to give up habituated behavior that demands following the rules and obeying laws when this keeps you from fulfilling your destiny.

Bertrand Russell observed that "from childhood upward, everything is done to make the minds of men and women conventional and sterile." This includes many of the edicts, both written and spoken, that you've been taught to observe as you move through life. Many of these rules are simply the *shoulds:* "You *should* do things the way we've always done things in this family," "You *should* keep quiet and do as you're told," "You *should* fit in and take the courses that the school offers," "You *should* take the advice of authorities, rather than have a different opinion," "You *should* want to continue living near family, instead of moving across, or out of, the country," and so on. All of these *shoulds* are designed to keep you from hearing a certain drumbeat, which, if further ignored, may lead to disastrous results.

Thoughtless obedience to rules and laws is both dangerous to society as a whole and an impenetrable obstacle in the way of your health and happiness. You see, your subconscious mind may be so programmed that you allow all of these memes or mind viruses to

51

dictate your options in life. If you recognize that you're a spokesperson for always obeying rules and laws and doing as you're told, you need to also recognize that you pass on mind viruses to others similar to the ones that are curtailing your own life. Some of the most heinous acts in human history have been performed under the umbrella of "the law" and "the rules." And many beliefs and opinions are merely excuses defended as rules or laws.

Listen to your own heart, and obey whatever is consistent with what you know to be the highest law of all. Subscribe to edicts that encourage you and others to be all that you're capable of becoming without interfering in any way with anyone else's God-given rights. In this *Excuses Begone!* attitude you'll never be limited by laws, rules, or *shoulds*. As the 18th verse of the Tao Te Ching states:

> *When the greatness of the Tao [God] is present,*
> *action arises from one's own heart.*
> *When the greatness of the Tao [God] is absent,*
> *action comes from the rules*
> *of "kindness and justice."*

Let the greatness of the Tao live in your heart and encourage you to act from that elevated place.

14. It's Too Big

The "It's too big" excuse is *so* big that it seems to plop on top of people and totally immobilize them. Perhaps surprisingly, this belief only needs to be reversed. If you believe that people are successful because they think big, for instance, I'm here to tell you that success demands small thinking! Bring this realization into your consciousness and you will have accessed the ability to think small and act on what once seemed to be big issues. Some of these include: being overweight, battling an addiction to legal or illegal substances, having an unwanted self-image, earning your Ph.D., building your new house, getting out of debt, fixing your relationship with your mother, or becoming more self-reliant.

Verse 63 of the Tao clearly and gently explains what I'm talking about:

> *Take on difficulties while they are still easy;*
> *do great things while they are still small.*
> *The sage does not attempt anything very big,*
> *and thus achieves greatness.*

These words may appear to be paradoxical, but they're the unquestionable response to this particular excuse.

As I write this, there's a 12-story structure being erected next door to my condo building. Admittedly, there had to be some big thinking on the part of those who imagined and designed this project. However, the actual creation of this beautiful new edifice is being accomplished in terms of what can be done right here, right now—one step, one brick, and one shovelful of dirt at a time. What a great metaphor to touch base with when you feel overwhelmed by the sheer scope of something. You cannot lose 50 pounds or quit smoking *in a single day,* get your Ph.D. *tomorrow,* or eliminate all debt from your life *forever* . . . such goals *are* too big when approached that way, and this makes it too easy to fall back into habituated ways.

The *Excuses Begone!* method invites you to challenge your thought patterns and encourage your own success. So acknowledge that you can't get the humongous things done today, but you *can* take that first step. While you can't receive your Ph.D. today, you can register for a course that begins next week, and that's all you can do regarding that lofty goal for now. Think small and accomplish what you can in the here-and-now. You can't quit drinking alcohol or smoking cigarettes for the next ten years, but you can refuse to give in to your addictions today, or even smaller, in this moment. That you *can* do. And that is precisely how all habituated thinking habits get changed: by thinking and acting small in the now moment and living the only way that anyone really does live—one minute, one hour, one day at a time. With this new consciousness, you can begin thinking in terms that encourage you to eliminate excuses and elevate success.

15. I Don't Have the Energy

Not having the vitality to fulfill your life purpose is part of a learned response. *I'm tired, I'm exhausted, I'm worn out,* and *I'm too weary* are just a few varieties of mind viruses that have infected you, consciously or not. They're generally an unintended excuse as opposed to a legitimate explanation for not doing the things you want to do. Accept the belief that you're lacking the energy to make significant changes in your life and you latch on to a flimsy, albeit very effective, strategy for maintaining some pretty slovenly habits.

You can hang on to any old and comfortable behavior patterns by using the tiredness excuse. *I'd love to get into shape, but I'm simply too exhausted to do what's required.* Or, *I want to become qualified for that new position, but I'm just too fatigued to go to school at night.* The belief in your "non-energy" becomes self-fulfilling until you have to rest again, because coming up with excuses is a very tiring practice!

The low-energy excuse is simply what I've seen myself and many others employ when we don't know how to overcome our own inertia, and I've found that when we really put it to the test, it doesn't hold up. I've witnessed an absence of energy turn into an avalanche of high energy in just an instant. When my children used to complain about being bored or too tired to move, for instance, all it took was a suggestion that we visit the water park, go shopping for a new bicycle, or do anything that they perceived to be fun, and they'd miraculously convert from weary to excited in a split second. And so it goes with all of us. We use the "I don't have the energy" excuse as a reason to hold on to an inert and pathetic way of being.

The antidote to this is to find a way to inject energetic thoughts into your everyday thinking. One of John F. Kennedy's biographers, Arthur M. Schlesinger, Jr., quoted the former President as saying: "I suppose if you had to choose just one quality to have, that would be it: vitality." Vitality isn't simply the amount of high-energy atoms you have swirling around inside of you; I consider it a way of thinking. You can learn to overcome the ennui of low-energy thinking and replace it with a way of processing the world that serves you in a positive, life-fulfilling way.

Low energy is by and large not a problem of body chemistry— it's a function of a long history of habituated thinking that needs excuses to stay the same. You can learn to practice more satisfying and vibrant thinking that will elevate your enthusiasm, and ultimately produce an energetic lifestyle filled with purpose. No matter what your chronological age is, you have the power to use your thoughts to elevate yourself to new levels of success, happiness, and health. *Excuses Begone!* thinking encourages you to spend your daily moments in aliveness, free of the old tiredness routine.

Refuse to cater to low-energy mental activity. Be determined to unquestionably place your thoughts not on what you can't do, but on what you intend to create. Stay in this mind-set and you'll never want to use the low-energy excuse again. Maintain your high-energy consciousness for what you want to accomplish, and watch it filter down to everyone you communicate with. High energy is infectious, and it originates with vital thinking that replaces those old mind viruses.

16. It's My Personal Family History

You've always had a place in your family, and regardless of your opinion about it, there's nothing you can do to change that. If you were the youngest and always ordered around, that's simply the condition of your early life. The fact is that your birth order (that is, being an only, oldest, middle, or youngest child) or any other familial sequencing—including being part of a blended family, having divorced or single parents, being adopted, having alcoholic parents, being of a low socioeconomic status, being racially mixed, or any of an endless combination of factors in your situation—is all in the past, and it's all over! Your relatives did what they did, given the circumstances of their lives. Acknowledge this, and then move into the present moments of life. Look at your family history as a blessing. Yes, a blessing! It's precisely what you had to go through to arrive where you are today.

The manner in which you were treated or even mistreated provided you with an opportunity to be a stronger, more self-reliant person. Early experiences aren't meant to be hidden behind when life isn't working out the way you want it to—they aren't reasons for staying stuck! But the family-history excuse has a huge following, so you have lots of company if you're using it to explain to yourself and others why you aren't who or what you want to be today.

The divorce that took place when you were a young child may have taught you many important life lessons, but more likely, you caught the cultural mind virus that goes something like this: *Coming from a broken family is a traumatic experience that causes irreparable damage to children.* A part of you believes and promotes this meme because it seems easier than exploring the pain that leads to a healthier and stronger mind-set. This part of you probably thinks that it's protecting you from that extremely painful childhood experience. Thus, you readily believe: *Chances are almost zero that I'll have a happy relationship after seeing how miserably my parents failed at marriage.*

You can change all of this by reminding yourself that you absolutely have the power to elevate your attitude and beliefs. Consciously take time to reimagine the family experiences you had in the early years of your life, regardless of how traumatic or troublesome they were at the time. You didn't have the ability as a child to make peace with them, but you do now. Be in a state of appreciation and gratitude for the parts of you that survived and still want to grow. Encourage them by refusing to settle for the "easy out" of excuses.

For example, the years I spent in foster homes gave me life experiences that helped me to teach self-reliance to millions of people. Watching my stepfather drink himself to death, along with living with the effects that alcoholism has on a family, was (and still is) a great lesson that keeps me on the path of sobriety today. The presence of scarcity and food shortages as a child gave me an appreciation for all that has come to me, and I can now assure the poverty-conscious part of me: *That was then, and this is now.*

Excuses Begone! encourages you to make peace with everything that transpired in your life, including the painful experiences of abuse, abandonment, and disrespect. By hanging on to these life-long, self-defeating thinking habits, you do yourself the following major disservices:

— **You get weaker and sicker.** Your biography can become your biology; that is, by clinging to old hurts or remembrances, you keep yourself in a place of attracting disease (or *dis-ease*) into your body. All of that anger, hatred, and anxiety is a vibrational match to the presence of serious illnesses . . . it's the Law of Attraction at work. If you think about what's missing or what you disliked about your early life, the universe will offer experiences that match what you're thinking. More of what was missing and what you disliked will continue to flow into your life in the form of disease.

— **You remain stuck in the past.** If you can't elevate the thoughts about your past that are causing you to remain unhappy, unsuccessful, and unhealthy, you stay stuck where you are. Keeping unfortunate memories from the past alive with remnants of the originating anger, hate, and sadness becomes a habituated way of processing life. For example, if you hated how your father didn't pay enough attention to you, and you use this to explain your adult self-consciousness, you're stuck in that long-held belief pattern.

You have the unquestionable ability today to elevate your consciousness to explore ways to relieve self-consciousness and attract people you want to be with, rather than continuing to explain to yourself that you can't attract those people because your father didn't pay enough attention to you. Remember, your life is happening *now*, in the present moment.

17. I'm Too Busy

Prior to writing this excuse catalog, I invited visitors to my Website to e-mail me their excuses for not living at the highest levels. In essence, I was interested in the excuses *they* have used in their lives. "I'm too busy" easily topped the list.

If you're overextended, know that you've chosen to be in this position. All of the activities of your life, including those that take up huge portions of your time, are simply the result of the choices you make. If your family responsibilities are problematic, you've opted to prioritize your life in this way. If your calendar is crammed, you've decided to live with a full schedule. If there are way too many small details that only you can handle, then this, again, is a choice you've made.

Surely, one of the major purposes of life is to be happy. If you're using the excuse that you're too busy to be happy, you've made a choice to be busy, and in the process, you've copped out on living your life on purpose. If you've substituted being busy for actively and happily fulfilling your destiny, you need to reexamine your priorities. Here is my mentor, Thoreau, on unexamined priorities: "Most men [or women] are engaged in business the greater part of their lives, because the soul abhors a vacuum, and they have not discovered any continuous employment for man's nobler faculties."

Don't let your soul languish unfulfilled in a vacuum. Instead, begin to examine just how you prioritize your life. All the details that occupy it keep you from a destiny that you're aware wants your attention. Contemplate these encouraging ideas to counter the "I'm too busy" excuse:

- *I know that I'm not a bad parent if I don't arrange my life to be available to chauffeur the children every day until they're adults.*

- *I'm allowed to say no to requests that keep me from having time to pursue my life purpose.*

- *There's no such thing as "a place for everything and everything in its place."*

- *There's no right way to do anything.*

- *I can have it my way because there are no absolute universal rules.*

It isn't my purpose to delineate all of the ways in which you can unload this excuse category. Practicing delegating, getting others to help out, and taking time for yourself are all possibilities as well. Thoreau is right in that there are nobler faculties you need to pay attention to, in addition to all of those other details that occupy your life. If you fear the part of your soul that's calling you to a higher place, then you'll probably continue to haul out this particular excuse.

Change this pattern by never saying or implying that you're too busy. Just drop it, and replace it with the following affirmation: *I intend to take time for myself to live the life that I came here to live, and to do it without ignoring my responsibilities as a parent, spouse, or employee.*

I learned this valuable technique from the great Vietnamese spiritual bodhisattva Thich Nhat Hanh in his book *Peace Is Every Step*. Recite these two lines anytime you can steal a few minutes from your daily schedule: "Breathing in, I calm my body. Breathing out, I smile." As Hanh writes: "'Breathing in, I calm my body.' Reciting this line is like drinking a glass of cool lemonade on a hot day—you can feel the coolness permeate your body. . . . 'Breathing out, I smile.'. . . Wearing a smile on your face is a sign that you are master of yourself." This simple exercise helps you prioritize your life with a sense of peace. Then you can look at precisely what it is you need to do in order to discard the busyness excuse.

There's a wonderful cartoon posted on the bulletin board of the yoga studio I frequent that summarizes the importance of saying "Begone!" to this popular excuse. Underneath the depiction of a doctor talking to an overweight patient, the caption reads: "What fits your busy schedule better, exercising 1 hour a day or being dead 24 hours a day?" That sums up my approach to this particular excuse. Practice elevating your thoughts every day, no matter how busy and important you are. Rather than insisting that you're too busy to exercise, for instance, think, *I exercise because I'm way too busy to take time for being sick.*

18. I'm Too Scared

Again, turning to my e-mail correspondents, here's what else they've told me: "I've always been afraid of being alone," "I'm scared of failing and I've been this way since I was a child," "It's a scary world and someone could hurt me," "I'm afraid something bad will happen to me or my family," "I'm afraid that someone will yell at me, and I can't handle criticism," and "I'm scared about being poor or losing my job and not being able to get another one." Clearly, fear is a biggie in the excuse catalog.

A way out of the "I'm too scared" thought pattern is offered in *A Course in Miracles.* I have a special love for this weighty tome that tells us there are only two emotions we can experience: *love* and *fear.* Anything that is love cannot be fear, and anything that is fear cannot be love. If we can find our way to stay in a space of love, particularly for ourselves, then fear is an impossibility.

I believe that fear is a mind virus that insists you're either a success or a failure, and it's passed from one mind to another until it becomes a habit. From an early age, you're taught to feel: *If I don't succeed at everything I attempt, then I'm a failure as a person— and I'm scared to death of having to live with such an awful label.* This virus is passed on to you from other minds who bought into the same logic . . . and it keeps on replicating, infiltrating, and spreading, until it becomes a habitual way of responding. You think fearful thoughts, and then you use those same thoughts to explain the deficiencies of your life. You act as if they're really true, when, in fact, they're nothing more than excuses.

Franklin D. Roosevelt's famous refrain from his first inaugural address, "The only thing we have to fear is fear itself," was crafted from Thoreau's observation that "nothing is so much to be feared as fear." These Tao men had it right—there really is nothing to be afraid of. When you begin applying the *Excuses Begone!* paradigm you'll find in Part III of this book, neither "I'm too scared" nor any of the other excuses in this chapter will hold up.

Here's a personal example: In the practice of Bikram yoga, which is a regular part of my life, there are two postures that require the practitioner to bend all the way over backward and hold the posture for a period of 30 seconds or so. When I first started this practice, I'd feel fear welling up in me as I attempted to grab my heels from a kneeling position. I remember saying to my instructor, "I just can't bend over backward; I feel as if I'm out of control. In fact, I've never even been able to do a backward dive into a swimming pool in my entire life." I had a great meme going here, which told me, *Going backward is scary—you'll lose control, you won't be able to see where you're going, you could fall, you could really hurt yourself,* and so forth. Each of these explanations was an excuse that kept me from mastering these new poses.

My fear was rooted in my absence of trust in myself based on a lifetime of mind viruses. When I shifted my mind from fear to love, however, a remarkable thing happened that freed me from the chains of that habituated thinking: I saw myself cradled in the arms of a loving presence. I then said something to myself that I'd never uttered before: "Wayne, you can do these two exercises; you are a Divine piece of the all-knowing intelligence. First, love yourself and trust in this wisdom, and then let go and let God." By moving to love, fear was impossible, and 60-plus years of excuse making went out the window.

Today, I enjoy demonstrating both the Camel and Fixed Firm postures for new students. Out of all 26 postures, these 2 give me the greatest sense of joy and accomplishment. As the saying goes: "Fear knocked on the door. Love answered, and no one was there."

Here's a recap an affirmation for each of the 18 most commonly used excuses. The affirmations will assist you in making a conscious effort to encourage yourself to elevate your beliefs, unquestionably!

1. **It will be difficult:** *I have the ability to accomplish any task I set my mind to with ease and comfort.*

2. **It's going to be risky:** *Being myself involves no risks. It is my ultimate truth, and I live it fearlessly.*

3. **It will take a long time:** *I have infinite patience when it comes to fulfilling my destiny.*

4. **There will be family drama:** *I would rather be loathed for who I am than loved for who I am not.*

5. **I don't deserve it:** *I am a Divine creation, a piece of God. Therefore, I cannot be undeserving.*

6. **It's not my nature:** *My essential nature is perfect and faultless. It is to this nature that I return.*

7. **I can't afford it:** *I am connected to an unlimited source of abundance.*

8. **No one will help me:** *The right circumstances and the right people are already here and will show up on time.*

9. **It has never happened before:** *I am willing to attract all that I desire, beginning here and now.*

10. **I'm not strong enough:** *I have access to unlimited assistance. My strength comes from my connection to my Source of being.*

11. **I'm not smart enough:** *I am a creation of the Divine mind; all is perfect, and I am a genius in my own right.*

12. **I'm too old (or not old enough):** *I am an infinite being. The age of my body has no bearing on what I do or who I am.*

13. **The rules won't let me:** *I live my life according to Divine rules.*

14. **It's too big:** *I think only about what I can do now. By thinking small, I accomplish great things.*

15. **I don't have the energy:** *I feel passionately about my life, and this passion fills me with excitement and energy.*

16. **It's my personal family history:** *I live in the present moment by being grateful for all of my life experiences as a child.*

17. **I'm too busy:** *As I unclutter my life, I free myself to answer the callings of my soul.*

18. **I'm too scared:** *I can accomplish anything I put my mind to, because I know that I am never alone.*

This concludes Part I. You've identified 18 of the most common excuses and have been introduced to reasons for removing habituated thoughts that have been holding you back from living life at the highest levels of success, happiness, and health. Now, in Part II, you'll find the seven principles that lead to a lifetime of no excuses!

THE KEY
EXCUSES BEGONE!
PRINCIPLES

*"Every mind must know the whole lesson for itself—
must go over the whole ground. What it does not
see, what it does not live, it will not know."*

— Ralph Waldo Emerson

INTRODUCTION TO PART II

Each chapter in Part II illustrates one of the seven principles of *Excuses Begone!* that I've personally explored and applied to my own life. Yet I'm leaving out any remnants of my scholarly research persona, and instead expressing my unbridled enthusiasm about what it feels like to live in this new way. While I'll share my discoveries with you, it's my hope that you'll share my excitement through your own experience. (I've included exercises at the end of every chapter that will help you put these life-changing principles into practice.)

CHAPTER 4

THE FIRST PRINCIPLE: *AWARENESS*

*"Thinking without awareness is the
main dilemma of human existence."*

— Eckhart Tolle

*"It's the awareness . . . of how you
are stuck, that makes you recover."*

— Fritz Perls

Lifelong, set-in-stone thinking keeps you stuck . . . often without your even realizing that you're stuck! Since this type of mental
activity can't lead you in a new direction, becoming aware must
be the first step to getting rid of your excuses forever.

Cultivating awareness is indeed the preliminary activity in the
"I-opening" experience of meeting your *authentic self.* Living your
life oblivious to your thinking patterns and beliefs, day after day,
year after year, is a habit that encourages and elevates your ego or

false self. Eckhart Tolle states that "awareness and ego cannot co-exist" because awareness encourages and elevates your authentic self to be the center of your life experience. Although the false and authentic selves are mutually exclusive, I believe that knowledge of both is valuable. The way I see it, if you're going to practice an *Excuses Begone!* life, your primary relationship needs to be 100 percent with your authentic self.

Who you truly are originated in a formless, invisible world. Scientists acknowledge that all particles (including you) emerge from an energy field of *no-thing-ness.* It's Spirit that gives life, and it's to Spirit that all life returns. There's very little room for ego here, since it clings to the false belief that you are your possessions and achievements. Becoming mindful of your true essence leads to awareness of your magnificence, your Divinity, and your unique power to create for yourself whatever you feel is your destiny here on this planet, beyond any and all excuses.

When awareness is your reality, you don't need to explain your shortcomings or missed opportunities. Instead, you transcend the pull of ego and move into a totally new dimension of higher consciousness. To put it simply and bluntly: if you don't realize that you no longer have to be stuck in your old thinking habits, then the habits will prevail and persist.

This chapter introduces you to what awareness of the elevated experience of life feels like.

From Excuses to Awareness

Breaking old habits requires noticing that you're creating impediments in your life, and that these impediments have become excuses for so-called limitations. For example, if you're averse to risk taking and tend to choose the safe or easy path, this has caused you to erect mental barriers. Such barriers are what I'm calling "excuses," and they give you a way out. So when it's time to try something new—or to take a step that might result in failing, becoming the butt of criticism, losing a contest or competition, or anything at all that puts you on the path toward becoming a stronger and more self-reliant person—you come up with the same old excuse and avoid the risk. This is all an exercise that starts and ends in your mind: it's habituated thinking you rationalize by saying that it was inherited, or foisted on you by well-meaning (albeit cautious) parents.

Simply being cognizant of your excuse making will open you up to vast arenas of new possibilities. You can begin this process by paying attention to the false part of yourself that *believes* in limitations. Simply observe the thoughts in your mind and the feelings in your body and note when they don't resonate with your authentic self. Yet you don't have to change or fix those thoughts and feelings. By becoming aware of your true being, you only need to pay uncritical attention to the ego self, and it will recede gradually and naturally in the light of your awareness. Remember, you're not just the temporary shell that you call your "body"— you're a Divine essence who is limitless, formless, and infinite.

When you notice your ego's chatter, you discover the ability to overcome long-established habits, and you begin to see all that you've been blinded to by excuse making. Awareness leads to your highest self; ego leads to your earthbound self. When you let the Divine grow within you, awareness will be what you bring to all aspects of your life.

As a Hindu devotee was once told: "The blossom vanishes of itself as the fruit grows, so will your lower self vanish as the Divine grows in you." Letting the Divine grow within you involves sincerity, service to others, kindness, and reverence for all of life. Endeavoring to become aware encourages authentic thoughts to grow and appear in your inner world, and so will your lower self vanish as the Divine grows within you.

Let me share with you how awareness has been such a boon for me personally as I've changed some long-held thinking patterns. In the opening chapters of this book, I described two big excuses (genetic and memetic) that many of us use to explain away what appears to be our failure to change the habits that plague us. As I read *The Biology of Belief,* the phrase *perception controls genes* kept attracting me. It triggered something in me that I hadn't considered before: the idea that the way I think about and perceive my world can overcome my DNA and my genetic inheritance.

This means that I can rewire my internal circuitry and process physical or health problems from an entirely new perspective. If I were to stay unaware of my built-in ability to influence my genetic programming, I'd be stuck believing that those things were outside of my control. So I've become increasingly aware that my mind has power over my environment—which means that when my body is off track, it's because my beliefs are off track. All my life I've heard that the one thing you can't change is your DNA, and I've always nodded in agreement. With my current awareness of the power of perception, however, a whole new world has opened up for me.

For example, I have a history of infection and discomfort in my chest and bronchial area, and I've tended to feel that this is an area of weakness to be concerned about. A minor sore throat appears, which proceeds to some coughing that then produces green phlegm, followed by some difficulty breathing, and I head out to purchase some antibiotics and go through the same old process until the infection and discomfort ultimately disappear. Yet since doing the research for this book, part of which involves putting into practice what I'm learning and writing about, I've moved into a new mental state. I now encourage myself to apply awareness rather than my old routine, and I seem to skip over those days of discomfort and the annoying antibiotics.

In fact, I'm approaching everything about my body with a new awareness. Rather than first reverting to ways I've used in the past to process early signs of a physical malady, these days I shift to a level that allows me to mentally suspend my ego and even my body. Then I tell myself something along these lines: "My perceptions [beliefs] control my environment [my body, which is the environment for all illness], my genetic structure, and my DNA. I have the power to see this situation differently than I used to. Inherent within me is the power to create an inner environment that isn't susceptible to illness or disease." When I know that I have an option of awareness, I'm able to send away a possibly painful episode.

I'm using all of the power that this approach holds to talk differently to my body, and not only with respect to potential bronchial infections. I'm also employing it with sore joints, muscle pulls, cramping in my calves, stiffness, and any of the multitude of physical inconveniences that crop up in a 60-something body that loves exercising—particularly swimming, running, walking, and doing yoga—on a daily basis. The key is to be aware that awareness itself is available rather than that same tired old ego-dominated approach. The reason why "awareness of awareness" is so powerful is that it immediately puts me in touch with a dimension of myself that knows: *here in awareness, all things are possible.* That statement leaves nothing out, including the ability to realign with Source and introduce my genes to a new set of beliefs.

Reading about and processing these cutting-edge scientific ideas triggered my entry into awareness. But it was my willingness to work on *applying* it where only old thinking habits previously resided that brought me to this new level where I feel as if I have an all-knowing friend with me at all times. This friend is awareness.

Here's another example of the power of awareness to alter some long-running thinking habits:

> Just being conscious of the fact that you are exercising can lead to better fitness. A recent Harvard University study, published in a February 2007 issue of *Psychological Science,* tracked the health of 84 female room attendants working in seven different hotels and found that those who recognized their work as exercise experienced significant health benefits.
>
> The women were separated into two groups: One learned how their work fulfilled the recommendations for daily activity

levels, while the other (the control group) went about work as usual. Although neither group changed its behavior, the women who were conscious of their activity level experienced a significant drop in weight, blood pressure, body fat, waist-to-hip ratio and body-mass index in just four weeks. The control group experienced no improvements, despite engaging in the same physical activities.

The study illustrates how profoundly a person's attitude can affect her physical well-being. So, if your daily routine keeps you on the move, start thinking of it as exercise. It may be enough to move you toward your fitness goals. (*Experience Life* magazine, May 2008)

Notice the opening line of this article: "Just being conscious of the fact that you are exercising can lead to better fitness." Awareness takes you out of your customary thinking.

As for me, since rewiring my thoughts to influence my body and even my DNA, my reality has changed significantly. Today when I feel a heaviness in my chest or get a sore throat, a pain in my joints, or even a headache, I first begin noticing without judgment. I simply pay attention by observing uncritically and allowing myself to focus in a curious, gentle manner. By turning toward my higher self, all of ego's fear begins fading in its light. By becoming aware—without falling into ego thoughts of pain, disruption, annoyance, or creating other mental barriers—the symptoms move on through my system, which is in a state of higher consciousness.

Where I once had a lifelong thinking habit that I didn't have the ability to adapt my genes to my perception or to rewrite my genetic codes with my beliefs, I now live in a new way. I gently notice my old ego-based beliefs whenever I note any kind of bodily malfunction. Awareness leads me to think totally differently, and it, sans ego, has put me into an instantaneous healing place on many occasions.

The Many Paths of Awareness

Awareness doesn't come to you exclusively from your intellect. Hafiz, a Persian poet in the Middle Ages, explains it this way: "Oh, thou who art trying to learn the marvel of love from the copybook of reason, I am very much afraid that you will never really see the point." In other words, studying these pages and memorizing the components of awareness will never replace experiencing it. So encourage yourself by spending time *noticing* where and what you're feeling in your physical body. This is the initial step toward achieving the consciousness that Lao-tzu speaks of: "The mystical techniques for achieving immortality are revealed only to those who have dissolved all ties to the gross worldly realm of duality, conflict, and dogma."

This is a telling message. I know that I see myself as an immortal being who receives guidance on awareness specifically because I let go and dissolve most of my ties to the world of duality, conflict, and dogma. The excitement of living from this perspective is beyond anything I can describe. It reminds me that I do exist in a place of *all things are possible,* and I apply this consciousness to all of my old thinking habits. I encourage you to do the same.

Know that you are a soul with a body rather than the reverse, and understand that this knowledge is your ticket to changing beliefs that keep you stuck in what Lao-tzu calls "your shallow worldly ambitions." Awareness will remind you of who you are capable of becoming. All that you need will appear when you're vigilant about replacing old thinking habits with it.

These days, the words *infinite possibilities* flash on my inner screen almost every waking hour. This phrase continually assures me that nothing is impossible if I can conceive of it, and if I'm willing to apply awareness rather than excuses. Awareness allows me to perceive possibilities rather than difficulties, to feel connected to my Source of being and see the outcome as working rather than failing. I feel a dazzling rush of excitement when I think about no longer employing all the tired excuses that were handed down to me from my family, my schooling, my religious training, my government, ad infinitum. The messages were similar: "These are your limitations," "This is what you can and can't do," "This is the real world of competition and pain and violence and fear and hatred," and so on. These ideas strongly influenced me, but I'm here to tell you that I now have a new and welcome outlook on the world of infinite possibilities.

When you simply become aware, you cease being a victim to endless mind viruses that seemingly prevent you from accessing your complete fulfillment. You no longer find it difficult to change those familiar thought patterns that prevent you from living at optimal levels of success, happiness, and health. You consciously enjoy the knowledge that memes or genes or anything else in the material world don't have absolute control over you . . . and who you can become is unlimited. Your first response to any troublesome life situation isn't one of the 18 excuse categories from the last chapter; rather, you shift to your awareness of awareness and tell yourself, "Hold on here. There's something beyond what I'm noticing, and I'm going to tap into it first."

Madame Blavatsky, who was instrumental in introducing Eastern religions to the West, encouraged this kind of thinking. Here's what she said on this subject: "Have patience, Candidate, as one who fears no failure, courts no success. Fix thy Soul's gaze upon the star whose ray thou art, the flaming star that shines within the lightless depths of ever-being."

Suggestions for Implementing an Awareness of Awareness

— Develop a mind-set that stays open to all possibilities. Refuse to rule out the ability to use awareness as your primary tool for combatting long-held thinking habits. By being open to it, you invite higher awareness in. As I've said throughout this chapter, with this new approach, *all things are possible, and that leaves nothing out.*

— Practice using awareness at your own pace, in your own way, in circumstances that crop up throughout your daily life. Practice *giving* rather than *asking* for more; practice *being nonjudgmental* and *offering help* where you previously offered criticism. Want what you want for yourself even more for someone else, and observe how much better you are at eliminating those old "me first" thoughts that have demanded your attention in the past.

— In childhood, repetition was something you most likely used to reinforce things you were mastering. (You can probably recall insisting on someone reading and rereading a book or story until you knew it by heart.) In that spirit, repeat this affirmation over and over to have it solidify; and move from your subconscious, habitual mind to the forefront of your conscious mind: *I let go of old ways of thinking, and I access awareness.*

— When you feel compelled to use an excuse, become aware that you no longer need to. Simply become aware of this new awareness.

CHAPTER 5

THE SECOND PRINCIPLE: ALIGNMENT

"[I]t is only by becoming Godlike that we
can know God—and to become Godlike
is to identify ourselves with the divine element
which in fact constitutes our essential nature,
but of which, in our mainly voluntary
ignorance, we choose to remain unaware."

— from *The Perennial Philosophy*, by Aldous Huxley

Ego-dominated excuses wouldn't exist if we were able to adopt Huxley's advice above, which paraphrases Plato, and perfectly sums up the value of this second *Excuses Begone!* principle. Were we to "become Godlike" and be steadfast in thinking in harmony with the universal Source of being (which is our essential nature), then we simply wouldn't need to employ ego-dominated excuses.

Alignment is a basic truth that functions as your personal code, unlocking the mystery of manifesting anything into your life. You can learn how to readjust your thinking so that it aligns with your essential nature and puts you in harmony with Source energy . . . this symmetry will allow whatever you'd like to flow to you. Stay aligned with Source, and enjoy exploring an excuse-free life.

At this very moment, you can begin to practice alignment. First, notice your thoughts, and watch out for any of those habitually misaligned ones. Then just implement a different way of thinking that replaces the old habit. When you shift your thinking to align with an awareness of your essential nature, the energy is actually measurable.

It turns out that we live in a universe that is all energy. Everything vibrates, and the frequency of those vibrations determines how everything appears, including our body, which senses our thoughts and has energy components that can be measured. Our physical universe and everything in it is a vibrating machine. The act of creation itself, bringing nonbeing into being, is a vibrational frequency. Personally, this realization has been an awesome awakening for me, leading to my knowing in my heart that I have the power to harmonize with the vibrational Source and can activate whatever I focus on. And I believe that this ability is within every being.

There's an invisible energy field from which everything originates. Through the first *Excuses Begone!* principle of awareness, you can realign with the same vibrational frequency of that energy field and access what I call "Divine guidance." Why? Because of what seems to be a law of the universe, two frequencies that are alike are attracted to each other, and those that are unalike *don't even recognize* each other. Staying vigilant and continuously monitoring all thoughts causes you to notice what frequency you're transmitting and receiving. When you perceive that a thought is out of alignment, you can correct it; by doing so, you activate Divine guidance because you're now thinking at the same frequency as Source energy.

In the words of Lao-tzu some 2,500 years ago: "Relinquish the notion that you are separated from the all-knowing mind of the universe. Then you can recover your original pure insight and see through all illusions. . . . The breath of the Tao speaks, and those who are in harmony with it hear quite clearly." Note that Lao-tzu urges us to see that this is a *recovering* project—that is, the rediscovery of our original nature—and that our goal is to simply harmonize with the Tao (God source) in our thinking. So how does the Tao think?

If you could measure such a thing, you'd see that Source energy is a creating, giving, abundant, loving, joyful, nonjudgmental, all-things-are-possible, invisible mechanism. It is always giving, always serving, always in endless supply. It isn't really doing anything, yet nothing is left undone. It manifests being from non-being at a certain frequency—your job is to align with this frequency while simultaneously disabling the old, slower, ego-dominated thought frequencies. Being stuck in lack, busyness, lost opportunities, bad luck, and so on is a misalignment with the frequencies of your original nature. I'm sure that you'd prefer being in a state of rapport with the all-creating Divine mind, as opposed to being stuck in the muck of excuses.

Excuses Are All Misalignments

Look back at Chapter 3 and consider what those 18 excuses I delineated say to you. Go down the list and you'll see that they all focus on what "can't" be done or why it has "never" happened. The only thing an excuse gives you is an option out of the life that you'd like to live. Words like *difficult, risky, can't, not strong, not smart, rules, too big,* and *too complicated* excuse you from being the kind of person you'd like to be and were destined to become. Now consider how Source energy seems to operate. Does it really seem that it's possible for God or Divine mind to think in "it can't be done" ways? Of course not.

The logic seems abundantly clear to me: *harmonize with energy that can do anything and everything, for this is your original nature.* Excuses are evidence that you've discarded a way of thinking that's all-powerful for one that's all-limiting. In other words, it's imperative that you decrease ego-dominated thinking (which offers you mostly excuses) in favor of thinking that's aligned with "all things are possible" ideas.

One of the most common kinds of habituated self-debilitating ideas concerns money. *I don't have enough money* is a misaligned thought because money is in inexhaustible supply in the world. There is so much of it, in fact, that it would be impossible to create a calculator large enough to even count it!

Now, in order to receive what's being transmitted, frequencies of thought have to match up. Thought energy is picked up by a receiver tuned to the same frequency, so if Source energy is transmitting at 95.1 FM, tuning in to 610 AM isn't going to bring you what you want to hear. Likewise, it's impossible to pick up on what universal Source energy is transmitting if you stay misaligned and don't change frequencies to tune in to it. Just sit for a moment and let these thoughts be received right now: *You came from a Source that has unlimited abundance. It is still generating that same idea today—you merely left it behind. But when you return to those frequencies of your Source, you'll start to recognize them again. They'll begin to sound familiar to you. And ultimately you'll be back in harmony, singing the music that you sang long before you acquired an ego and began your journey of misalignment.*

While I'm using the example of money here, this logic applies to all the habitual thoughts or excuses you use to explain why your life isn't the way you claim to envision it. Therefore, *I need to be healed* is a vibrational match to *I don't have access to perfect health, and God is withholding His healing power from me.* You are a physical extension of the Source of life, and that Source is nothing but well-being. But you can't access this well-being when you vibrate to a different frequency!

I need someone to live up to my expectations and to love me in the way I want to be loved in order to be happy is another common misaligned thought. Yet Source energy is only about love. As Meister

Eckhart wrote in the 13th century: "All God wants of thee is for thee to go out of thyself . . . and let God be God in thee." So come on, wake up! Just let Source energy *be* Source energy in you. And Source energy has no excuses built into it. It simply says that you are love and you are loved, and all you have to do to get this is to be a vibrational match to love. Or as the Prayer of Saint Francis puts it: "Where there is hatred [or anything else that is not of Source], let me sow love." When you become that vibrational match and align yourself in this way, you'll see your desires begin to manifest for you immediately.

Alignment Is Awareness in Action

You may recall from the previous chapter that awareness is a representation of your highest self, the self that truly knows that it is a physical extension of the Divine, the invisible Source of all. Alignment represents movement into this state of awareness. *Alignment* is a verb—it connotes action, be it the action of literally changing old thinking habits so that they match up to your awareness, or the actual shifting of behavior so that you think and act as a God-realized *Excuses Begone!* being.

When you become aligned, your thoughts are no longer focused on what you don't want but rather on what you intend to manifest as a co-creator with Source. The best way to begin retraining your mind is to consciously think in aligned ways, so consider the following:

- Your universal Source of being never thinks in terms of what is missing. *Do you?*

- It never thinks in terms of what it can't have or do. *Do you?*

- It never thinks in terms of what has never happened before. *Do you?*

- It never thinks in terms of what others will think, say, or do. *Do you?*

- It never thinks in terms of bad luck or the way things have always been. *Do you?*

Every time you have a thought that extends to a conversation with others about what is missing, what shortages you have, your bad luck, what always has been, how others don't understand you, and so forth, you're practicing a misaligned/excuses mentality. But remember that your mission is to shift into the action state of realigning.

That reminds me of a story I was told by a minister on Maui. It seems that there was a family who had a very rambunctious five-year-old, and the parents were deeply concerned that he might inadvertently cause harm to his new baby brother. One night while they looked into the nursery to ensure the safety of their sleeping infant, they overheard their eldest son ask his brother, "Would you please tell me what God is really like? I think I'm forgetting." Indeed, most of us have forgotten what our Source of being is like, and it's particularly noticeable in the excuses we habitually make.

It's my contention that the universe not only will, but *must* provide you with what you conceive of. So if you complain about what's missing from your life—including the money that you believe to be in short supply—you'll be offered experiences that match that energy. When you say, "I love my job, but I'll never get rich at it," you're aligning with a frequency that will give you what you think. This is why, I believe, the rich often get richer . . . it's certainly been true for me since I left poverty behind me some 60 years ago.

By staying focused on what I intend to create, by believing that the universe is all-providing, and by knowing that I'm worthy of the unlimited beneficence of the Source of being, I just keep attracting prosperity to me. And by being unattached to what shows up, which means that I have no desire for more and more, I'm able to let it go easily. What remains a mystery to so many remains a simple truth to me.

Stay in a state of gratitude, and let the awesome yet unexplainable Tao proceed to do nothing and yet leave nothing undone. Rather than asking for more—which implies shortages and, therefore, creates a vibrational match to more shortages—focus on what you have and how thankful you are for everything that has shown up in your life.

To that end, keep in mind a "happiness index" that was recently taken for different countries around the world. It turns out that Nigeria, which is one of the poorest of nations, with the least modern of conveniences, came in at number one for reports of happiness among the people there. The U.S. ranked 46 out of 50, despite having one of the highest standards of living in the world. Apparently, the emphasis in Nigeria isn't on the mantra of the ego, which demands more, more, more. Emphasizing needing *more* has built within it the idea of shortage, lack, and *I don't have enough.* Consequently, when you think *more,* you become a vibrational match to experiencing more shortage in your life . . . like it or not!

Thinking Alignment at All Times

When you're thinking about the principle of alignment, keep in mind that Source energy is ever present, and that you always have the power to bring yourself into harmony with who you really are. And who you really are is a higher awareness than your earthbound form. Just this simple idea—that you're not an ego-based self but rather Divine energy in physical form—will help readjust your energy. Once you recognize your Divinity, you'll shift out of misaligned thought patterns. Such thinking focuses on what's wrong or missing, what others have told you are your limitations, what always has been, what used to be, and so on.

Since everything comes in response to the vibration of energy, shift out of the lowered vibrations and into the vibration of Source. *It's already here; I just need to connect to it. Nothing can stop my creative ideas from materializing. I've banished all doubt. I'll soon be seeing evidence of my manifestations everywhere . . .* now this is a new kind of thinking. While it may sound too simplistic and naïve for you, I'm encouraging you as strongly as I know how to give this retraining of your mind a chance.

Note that the strength of nonphysical energy is flowing everywhere. It's in you; but it's also in every tree, every flower, every bug, every planet, and in everything that you want to attract to your life. The nonphysical energy is pure positive oneness, which only your thoughts can disconnect from or misalign with. It flows everywhere at once; and it's always creating, always loving, and always animating life. The only thing that keeps it from working for you is a belief that it can't, it won't, or it never has before—in other words, your excuses.

The tremendous value of noticing the alignment of your thoughts will rapidly appear in your awareness. You can summon Source energy whenever you slip into a misalignment: just return to possibilities, manifestations, and your own sense of feeling good (which is just another way of feeling the presence of God).

When you find it difficult to move into this alignment attitude, put more attention on your *feeling-self* concerning your desires. For example, if that same old shortage of money surfaces, you may find that you can't stop yourself from being upset about the fact that you still believe that more cash would be your proof that this is working. Try something different, and let the energy of what you're feeling reveal what's blocking your alignment. Even if you have to borrow a few hundred dollars just to carry around with you and get the sensation of abundance, feeling prosperous, safe, secure, and positive concerning the flow of money will gradually align you with an abundant Source. This has been my way since I was a little boy.

I've attracted money into my life because I always felt prosperous and deserving. That feeling motivated me to act, and I loved carrying groceries or collecting soda-pop bottles or mowing lawns. My little bank account was growing while my brothers and friends spoke so often about not having enough cash. Today, I'm still mowing lawns and collecting soda-pop bottles, only on a much larger stage, and prosperity has never failed to flow into my life. I know in my heart of hearts that the journey from despair to hope and on to prosperity and abundance can be achieved with realigned thinking. I know because I've done it for a lifetime, and I trusted this under circumstances where it never could have been predicted that I'd emerge with unlimited prosperity as my calling card.

No one else can do this realignment exercise for you. You must decide to stay in the feeling of love, prosperity, wellness, or whatever you desire, and let that feeling just flow through you. And remember that you get what you think about, whether you want it or not. Remain thoughtfully in the field of infinite possibilities rather than your negative emotions—fear, worry, hate, and shame are indicators of separation from your authentic self in the present moment. When you come back to your authentic self, it will work full-time to deliver to you whatever you think about.

Silently repeat the following: "I get what I think about, and I am choosing from here on in to think in harmony with my Source of being until it is habitual!" This is alignment.

Suggestions for Implementing a
Realigned Way of Being

— Test your ability to access Divine guidance. Think in harmony with Source energy by taking on a small project. Choose any subject—bumblebees, lightbulbs, feathers, pennies, anything at all—and do nothing but keep it in your mind. Generate pure positive energy around this topic: See the feather or the penny showing up, and feel good about this occurrence. Let your mind be at living peace with this item, and then become an observer rather than a demander and notice what happens.

By aligning with a field of possibilities in a nonjudging, non-demanding, yet totally accepting way, you'll notice the manifestation into your life space of that which you're aligned with in your thoughts. Release any ideas that you're impotent when it come to co-creating your life.

— Practice catching yourself when you're engaged in the habit of negative thinking. Monitor any thought that expresses, *It can't, It won't,* or *It's not my luck;* and change it to an aligned thought such as, *It will, It must,* or *It's already here and I know it will arrive on schedule with Divine timing.* Change these misaligned thoughts (excuses) one minute, one hour, one day at a time.

— Affirm: *I am aligned with my Source in all of my thoughts, and with God, all things are possible,* continuously as many times as you can in a five-minute period. The act of repetition helps the thought become a habituated method of alignment. Soon you'll emphatically say, "Excuses, be . . . gone!"

CHAPTER 6

THE THIRD PRINCIPLE: *NOW*

"Memories of the past and anticipation of the future exist only now, and thus to try to live completely in the present is to strive for what already is the case."

— Alan Watts

You've heard it many times, so often in fact that it has become a cliché: *Live in the present. The now is all there is. Forget about the past; it's over. Don't worry about the future; there is only today.* While these are familiar refrains, the truth is that living in the now is an elusive activity for virtually everyone. It may be easy to say, but it's very tricky to do day in and day out. And yet, Alan Watts is absolutely correct in the above quotation when he states that it "already is the case." This is why living in the present moment is so baffling.

Think about the past and you're not living in the now . . . but the now is the only time available for thinking about the past! Live in anticipation of the future and you're admonished for not being here now . . . but now is all you have for engaging in that delicious "futurizing." Thus, as Alan Watts reminds you, you strive for what *already is*. To be in the now is really your only option. But the real question isn't how to *live* in the now, it's how to *use* the now by being present—rather than wasting it on reflections of the past or concerns about the future. And if you carefully examine the 18 categories of excuses detailed in Chapter 3, you'll discover that none of them applies if you master the art of being present.

Ego, Excuse Making, and the Elusive Now

After spending several days preparing to write this chapter, I was trying to focus on its significance when I decided to go for a long swim in the ocean. As I walked toward the water, I noted that I felt some tension in my solar-plexus region. It wasn't anything serious—it was just the discomfort I often feel when I have many things to do or decisions to make. At the moment I was about to dive in, my thoughts went back to the reading I'd just finished on the psychology of the now. I decided to see if I could totally immerse myself in the moment (which, of course, meant that I was in fact striving for what "already is the case," since I have no other moment than this one), only this time, I'd be fully present, letting everything just be. I wouldn't worry about the ache in my chest, think about how cold the water would be or which direction the current was flowing, or rehash all the things I had on my current to-do list. I'd simply be in the now.

I indeed let everything else go and stayed focused on the instant, the place, and the surroundings. And something strange and wonderful happened: My chest stopped hurting, I loosened up, all of my anxiety dissolved, and I felt totally energized. For the next 60 minutes or so, I moved through the water staying 100 percent present. The moment I decided to just be there completely, with all other thoughts pushed aside, the discomfort I was experiencing disappeared. Moreover, I had the most peaceful swim I've ever had, and I emerged from the water fully refreshed.

My conclusion is that the present moment is an antidote for the pain and difficulties we experience, which we habitually try to soothe with rationales and explanations. When we plunge ourselves 100 percent into the now, experiencing it and nothing else, we're on an *Excuses Begone!* journey, with no need for all of those old habituated thinking patterns.

In fact, excuses are simply what you've developed to explain *now* moments that are tangled in the past or future. If you're truly in that blissful presence of the now, there's no desire to alter what is. When your sentences express that "it's going to be difficult . . . it will take a long time . . . I'm not smart enough . . . I'm too old," you're wasting a present moment with excuses from a not-now moment! And when are you having these thoughts? You guessed it—the only time you have a thought is in the now. So if your present moment is being used up replaying why present-moment thinking is incorrect (making excuses), is it available for you to do something constructive? Obviously not!

All excuses are avoidance techniques to keep you from taking charge and changing your thinking habits. If you weren't rehashing your excuses but were instead immersed in the now, you'd be experiencing your own form of the bliss and healing that took place for me during my magical swim. You see, when I removed ego from the moment, I stopped thinking about myself and focused on being fully present—and then I was able to be truly *here* without ego's excuses. I had plenty of explanations for the tension in my chest, but when I moved totally into the now with no other thoughts, the excuses disappeared along with the pain.

The ego is a false self that believes in its separation. It strives to acquire and to achieve, and it's constantly in search of more. Just as it can't coexist with awareness and alignment, it can't survive in the now. When you luxuriate in the moment, it's impossible to ask for anything else, let alone more. The essence of living in the present is total acceptance of precisely what is here. Your mind doesn't wander to what used to be, what ought to be, or what's missing; and you don't conjure up excuses. Rather, you have a heightened awareness of experiencing your highest self.

You also feel a deep sense of connection to God, Who isn't doing anything differently than God was doing an hour or a century ago, or will be doing a millennium from now. Your Source energy is always only here and now. It doesn't know how to be any other way. It has no plans, no regrets, no worries about the future, no guilt over the past. It simply is. And what is God doing? Nothing. And what does God leave undone? Nothing.

By staying in the now and in a state of gratitude for all that is and all that you are, you tame the ego and enter a state where excuses cannot even be considered. What excuse do you need when you're fully present? None. Of what use is ego, that false self, when you're with your Source in the moment? Don't use up the now with thoughts of regret or worry; the experience of higher awareness is your reward. When the ego's in control, virtually every thought is making an excuse, focusing on what always has been or what you fear always will be. But when you befriend the present moment, you say good-bye to that troublesome ego.

The issue isn't whether you choose to live in the now or not, because the basic truth is that it's the only thing that's ever available to live in. The past all occurred in the now. The future, which never comes except as a present moment, is all that's available. *The real issue is how you choose to use up the precious moments of your life.* You can choose higher awareness and suspend ego-dominated past/future thoughts, eliminating your reliance on excuses. Full immersion into the essence of the now is when you truly come face-to-face with your Source of being. This is the great value of learning to become fully present.

Befriending the Now

Often, the now is seen by ego as simply a means to an end, something to be endured to get to a future point. This means never getting to be fully here in the moment, since you're using it up anticipating where you'll be in the future. Of course the future is endlessly always just ahead of you—as thoughts in your head—setting you up for a life of striving rather than arriving.

However, this particular course in *Excuses Begone!* takes quite a different stance. Rather than wasting time being annoyed because there's so much planning to do for the future, stop and remind yourself to *Be Here Now,* as my friend Ram Dass suggested in the title of his famous book. To do so, *befriend* the now. See it as your ally—the only place you've ever been, or ever will be, and do a brief meditation reminding yourself what this life experience is all about.

One of my favorite techniques to bring me squarely into alignment with the present is to imagine what all of God's beautiful creatures do in every moment of their existence. They're not concerned with their demise; they bask in the exhilaration of the now. Every moment is fully experienced. I don't see any creatures seemingly hating what they're doing, cursing their lot in life, or arguing with themselves or each other over what is. They don't make life an enemy and use up their precious moments in a state of anxiety or depression.

Years ago I was privileged to take part in a safari in the northern region of South Africa. The other members of the group and I were gathering for dinner one evening when we noticed six or seven zebras grazing outside our tent. As we got a closer look, I noticed something that I've used ever since to remind me to maintain a friendly relationship with the now rather than treating it as an obstacle to endure on the way to somewhere else.

One of the zebras had been attacked during the night, and its right hindquarter and leg looked as if it had been chewed on by a lion looking for a meal. This beautiful animal seemed to be peacefully grazing, completely in the moment, even though one of its legs had almost been chewed off the night before. I thought that if that animal was capable of being fully present under such conditions, how could I suffer anxiety over what might or might not happen in the future, or be upset about what took place in the past? That zebra seemed to be saying, "This is the only moment

I have. This is what is, and I'm going to live fully in each instant until I leave this plane of existence."

While this is an extreme example, it always serves to help me—particularly whenever I'm leaning toward those excuses that I've often employed when I slip into making the present moment an enemy rather than a constant companion. I think of that astonishingly beautiful yet maimed zebra, and I get myself right back to the now. And I'm there in such a way that I don't use it up by being upset over a past event or worrying about what's coming up.

Our relationship to the present moment defines our relationship to life itself. One of the greatest insights I've ever had concerns my experience of time as the ultimate illusion. I think about it in this way: Whatever has happened in the past—no matter how many years, centuries, or millennia ago—all took place in the now. Just now. There's no way to experience anything other than in the precious present. Thus, the idea that it happened in the past must be an illusion, since everything only gets experienced now. The "time thing" is a grand illusion.

The same logic applies equally to the future—whatever we fantasize about happening then will also only take place in the now. All we get is *now-now-now*. Time is what we seem to be measuring with wristwatches, clocks, and calendars; but in fact it's nothing more than a series of present moments.

The message, then, in this *Excuses Begone!* paradigm is that being in the now will help you overcome all of your explanations for why you aren't living at your highest level. Your relationship to life itself reflects your relationship to the present moment, so if your head is filled with frustrating or angry thoughts about what isn't happening or the way the world looks to you, you're not going to have a very good relationship with life. Yet a dysfunctional relationship with life is really nothing more than a dysfunctional relationship with the present moment. Again, *life only gets lived in the now.*

Rather than seeing your present moment as an obstacle, see it as the supreme miracle. "Wayne, this is the only moment you have," is a sentence I often say to myself to keep me on friendly terms with the now. Think about that: *the only moment you have.* When you realize the significance of this, you'll immediately want to shift into a state of awe and gratitude for it, regardless of what is transpiring. I do this frequently in my yoga practice, particularly when I'm challenged by a difficult posture. Balancing on one leg and holding the other one straight out with my hands cupped beneath the ball of my foot is a challenge that leads me to murmur, "Be here now, Wayne. There's a time for being exhausted, and there will be a time for resting, but it's not here yet, so just stay in the present moment." And of course it always passes, but the next moment that shows up, amazingly, also shows up as a now . . . and the next. And so it goes with every experience of life.

Removing Judgment

I've discovered that I have greater success with being fully present when I remove judgment from what I'm experiencing. Rather than making an event a bad or a good experience, I find myself simply being in the "isness" of the moment; that is, what I'm feeling is much more helpful than why it isn't what I think it should be. This is called *allowing* rather than *resisting* what is. Even if I wish to change the moment, it's far more useful to allow it without any judgment and then notice everything I can about it.

The more I stay out of my good-thought/bad-thought routine, the more I'm able to just be with it. I love to observe the instant without any judgment. Birds simply allow whatever comes their way, no matter if the wind picks up or the rain falls, and I work at being like one of those fabulous creatures. The way I do so is to ask myself this question: "What's happening right here and right now, independent of my opinion about it?" Then I notice all that I can take in—the sky, the wind, the sounds, the light, the insects, the temperature, the people, the judgments . . . everything. I stay free of opinions and just let myself be. In these moments, I don't need an excuse for anything.

Even while I sit here and write, I'm practicing being present and simply allowing the words to flow through my heart to my hand and onto the page with a total absence of judgment. And when I eat my lunch, I work at just being present in a state of gratitude for my food and the experience of eating, rather than using those moments to think about all that I have to do in the evening or passing judgment on the taste, color, or smell of my lunch experience. I try to keep in mind that whenever I react against any form that life takes in the present moment, I'm treating the now as some kind of impediment or even as my enemy.

As a child you knew how to be totally present. I encourage you to become an observer of little children. Notice how they don't react to every single disturbance in their world and how they're in the moment, and then in the next moment, and so on. You can use this kind of nonjudgment to practice your new explanation-free identity. Total immersion in the present, without judging—that is, simply allowing yourself to be—is a great way to rid yourself of these long-held thinking habits that I'm calling "excuses."

Be without judgment and you'll never feel the need for some tiresome excuse to use up your precious seconds, such as *It's never happened before . . . I'm too old . . .* or *It will take a long time.* Instead, you'll be in the now, welcoming your constant present-moment companion, your Source of being, which knows nothing of excuses and doesn't know how to be anywhere but here, now. As one of my spiritual predecessors, Dale Carnegie, once wrote: "One of the most tragic things I know about human nature is that all of us tend to put off living. We are all dreaming of some magical rose garden over the horizon—instead of enjoying the roses that are blooming outside our windows today."

Become one in the present with all of the roses that show up in your life.

Suggestions for Implementing
Present-Moment Awareness

— Practice becoming aware of your reactions when someone introduces any kind of mental disturbance into your life. Where do your thoughts take you? What do you think about in that instant? You'll probably find that your thoughts are projections into the past or the future, so bring yourself back to the now. As you're receiving the disrupting information, ask, *How am I feeling right now?* instead of *How am I going to feel later?* or *How did I feel back then?* By giving yourself a gentle reminder in the moment of your discomfort, you'll bring yourself back to what you're experiencing now. Watch as your discomfort dissolves when you return to the present. Just keep practicing bringing yourself back to the here-and-now, and remember as you do so that this is your relationship to life. Accept the present moment and find the perfection that's untouched by time itself.

— Give yourself the luxury of learning present-moment living by adopting the following two practices, making them a regular part of your daily life:

1. *Meditation.* Get rid of the excuses you've used that it's too difficult, you don't have the time or energy, and so forth. Begin today, practicing any form of meditation that appeals to you. You'll discover that you become adept at allowing interfering thoughts to flow through in the now, rather than trying to stop or change them.

2. *Yoga.* Find a studio and give yourself the opportunity to experience this ancient practice. The word *yoga* means "union," and the practice helps you rejoin your Source and free yourself from many of your useless, habitual thoughts. Yoga helps you look into your soul and be present. You'll experience the oneness of everything . . . you'll find peace rather than excuses.

97

— Repeat this affirmation: *I choose to stay fully present in the now, and this is the only place that I will come to know God.* By repeating this to yourself in silence for a five-minute period, you reinforce the importance of being a present-moment person. Repetition is crucial! Make this a regular practice and it will ultimately become your way of being.

— Stay present: every second, every minute, and every hour. Every day of your life is full of present moments of infinite value. You won't find God yesterday or tomorrow—your Source is always only here, now.

CHAPTER 7

THE FOURTH PRINCIPLE: CONTEMPLATION

"Contemplation is the highest form of activity."

— Aristotle

Every discovery of something new involves the crucial concept of contemplation. Think about airplanes weighing hundreds of tons flying around the world in relatively short periods of time. A century or so ago they didn't exist, but then the mechanics of flight were discovered. By generating a high rate of speed and designing wings that forced the air to push upward, lo and behold, heavier-than-air objects were staying aloft. When the Wright brothers arrived at Kitty Hawk, they hadn't been focusing on how things stayed on the ground; rather, they'd been contemplating the elevation of things moving in the air. So because they and others like them were willing to seriously think about something that didn't yet exist, air travel was brought into our reality system.

Contemplation is the mental activity behind all inventions— indeed, behind all of creation. Consequently, I urge you to become fully conscious of how you choose to use your mind as you study this fourth *Excuses Begone!* principle and its relationship to action. It's important that you understand that you can create the life you desire by concentrating on what you wish to attract. Once you master the ideas surrounding this concept, you won't want to use your mind for the purpose of excuse making. Instead, you'll prefer to use it to really consider what you want to manifest into your life and then visualize it as coming true.

The principle of contemplation is also what motivates human progress in cultural, political, and social contexts. For example, the idea of slavery being a horrible stain on the spiritual nature of humankind was realized by one person first, and then another, until the practice was finally abolished. The idea of women having the same right to vote as men was also conceived in a few minds before becoming a reality. These notions were *contemplated* first, and their destiny fits this sentiment from Victor Hugo: "There is nothing more powerful than an idea whose time has come."

Contemplation and Attraction

The excuses you tend to rely on probably include some ideas that you've contemplated throughout your life to date. Yes, even thinking *It will be difficult . . . I can't afford it . . .* or *I don't deserve it . . .* is engaging in what Aristotle called "the highest form of activity." The more you ponder the impossibility of having your desires show up, complain about life's unfairness, and get upset about what continues to manifest, the more those very things define your reality. That's because whatever you focus on invariably shows up in your life—be it what you want or what you *don't* want. So if you're always thinking or talking about what's wrong with your life, then you're attracting exactly what you don't desire.

Choosing an *Excuses Begone!* approach means that you absolutely refuse to participate in the self-defeating rhythm that I just touched on. You learn to move into a new realm where your thoughts are viewed as potential realities, and it's your sacred duty to contemplate only that which originates from your authentic self. This is something you can begin to work on right away.

I learned a long time ago from one of my mentors, Abraham Maslow, that self-actualizing people never use their minds to think about what they don't wish to attract. They don't worry about an illness getting worse, an absence of funding, a downturn in the economy affecting them, a negative outcome in a business venture, their children getting into trouble, and so on. Their minds focus on the conditions they wish to produce—then the lucky break, the right people or circumstances, or the synchronistic opportunity somehow presents itself as a result of their contemplation. We all become what we think about, so it's pretty important to pay attention to those thoughts.

And keep in mind what Aldous Huxley once noted: "Contemplation is that condition of alert passivity, in which the soul lays itself open to the divine Ground within and without, the immanent and transcendent Godhead." It's as if by thinking about what you desire, you release a zillion little invisible yet alert worker bees who guide you in the act of creation. Rather than being focused on a lame excuse, you use your mind to align with the all-knowing "transcendent Godhead." And when you use your mind in this way, miracles begin to show up.

This makes me think about something that recently happened to my daughter Serena. After graduating from the University of Miami, she and her friend Lauren were excited about creating a television show focusing on healthy eating, cooking, and general living geared toward their age group. We could all easily imagine Serena and Lauren hosting the show, and they went so far as to write a proposal and practice presenting the idea in a TV format. Unfortunately, they didn't seem to be able to find the right person or agency to represent them.

I asked Serena to contemplate herself surrounded by what she and Lauren wanted to attract, and to discard excuses such as, *It will be difficult . . . It's never happened before . . . It's too big . . .* or *I'm too young.* I reminded her to just keep contemplating, because that's the highest form of activity. Neither of us anticipated the way this would work out. But to understand, you first need a bit of history.

About 15 years ago, my daughter's best friend, Jesse Gold, and her family spent an evening with us in our summer apartment on Maui. That night, seven-year-old Serena had the entire gathering in tears one moment and laughing hysterically the next as she entertained us with her natural acting ability. Jesse's father, Harry, even wrote an agreement saying in effect that when Serena came to Los Angeles to become an actress, he'd like to represent her. He signed this spirit-of-the-moment contract and gave it to my wife, who kept it—unbeknownst to Serena—all these years.

Back to the present. A decade and a half had passed, and I was running late for a meeting in Burbank to discuss a television show with some producers. The traffic was heavy, I had difficulty finding a parking spot, and it felt as if nothing was going right with respect to the timing of this appointment. As I finally entered the lobby of the building where the meeting was to take place, the elevator door began to close as I approached. Thankfully, however, someone held it open.

I breathed a sigh of relief as I headed to my meeting on the 14th floor. And that's when I noticed that Harry Gold, who happens to be one of the top talent agents on the West Coast, was the person who was holding the elevator door open for me! Although we hadn't seen each other in years, Harry insisted that I stop to say hello to Jesse, who was working part-time in a restaurant in that same building while she pursued her career. We all hugged, laughed, and marveled at the set of circumstances that brought Harry and me together at that moment, in that elevator. And when I called Serena's mom later, she pulled out that little contract written in jest some 15 years ago.

By contemplating herself surrounded by the conditions she wished to attract, I believe that my daughter created an alignment that caused me to arrive late for that appointment at precisely the right moment that Harry could hold the elevator for me. Coincidence? Maybe. But what a beautiful coincidence. So many things had to appear to go wrong in order for all of this to manifest. Serena has now been able to welcome an opportunity for producing her television show, with representation for her idea by someone who agreed to do so in writing when she was a seven-year-old . . . someone who was as close to her as her own family was when she was a little girl.

I'm not the least bit concerned about the outcome of Serena's adventure. The point is that when you engage in the act of active contemplation, you set in motion a powerful force—you allow yourself to be lived by the great universal mind or Tao. I have no doubt that as my daughter continues her contemplative inner work, eschewing any excuse patterns and keeping all of her mental activity on what she intends to manifest, she'll see this kind of occurrence showing up regularly. What she does with it and where it will go are all wrapped up in what she continues to contemplate.

The Mechanics of Contemplation

Both Aristotle and Aldous Huxley offer us wonderful insights regarding the principle of contemplation. They both explain how the very act of reflecting on an idea, any idea, sets the process of creation into action—this is an integral component of living an *Excuses Begone!* life. As we know, Aristotle wrote: "Contemplation is the highest form of activity." And Huxley hit it on the head when he reminded us that the very process allows our soul to open to the Divine guidance that operates within us and everywhere in the universe simultaneously.

I've also been greatly influenced on this subject by a brilliant scholar named Thomas Troward. In 1910 he delivered a series of lectures that became books, which forever changed the way we look at the process of creation and manifestation. His writings can help us understand the power of contemplation, particularly in relationship to creation itself. I urge you to read his remarkable treatise, *The Creative Process in the Individual*.

In the Foreword, Troward writes: "In the present volume I have endeavored to set before the reader the conception of a sequence of creative action commencing with the formation of the globe and culminating in a vista of infinite possibilities attainable by every one who follows up the right line for their unfoldment." In the subsequent pages, he relates that the entire cosmos was created by self-contemplation, and infinite possibilities are available if you follow a pertinent sequence of creative action. This is all attainable for whoever is willing to follow "up the right line."

Troward asks you to get the steps of the creative process clearly into your mind as they relate to contemplation, and then watch excuses melt away and see the results of your efforts. Here is a summary of the four-part sequencing, or right line, for your consideration:

1. Spirit is created by self-contemplation. The process of moving from nonbeing to being involves an invisible Source, which we call "Spirit," deciding to expand into the world of form. This is God expressing Himself/Herself in all material things. Thus, coming from their originating nature, everything and everyone is a result of Spirit contemplating itself and expressing its inherent life, love, light, power, peace, beauty, and joy as a part of the material world.

2. So what it contemplates itself as being, it becomes. Contemplation by Spirit results in the manifestation of what is being contemplated. Troward goes to great lengths in his book to explain the Divine ideal and how the very cosmos had to come into being as a result of how the originating Spirit (Tao or God) engaged in self-contemplation for the purpose of expressing life.

3. You are individualized Spirit. Here's where you once again are urged to recognize your own Divinity. You too were materialized from nonbeing (Spirit) to being (form) by the self-contemplation of Spirit itself. And Spirit itself is oneness, indivisible. Since you are a piece of God, so to speak, the following conclusion is offered by Troward:

4. **"Therefore, what you contemplate as the law of your being becomes the law of your being."** And he goes on to state that you must use your creative power of thought to maintain your unity with Spirit rather than to create a separate sense of self that is cut off from Spirit and suffers from poverty and limitation. That is to say, as long as you're able to use your power of contemplation and stay in harmony with how Spirit contemplates itself, you have precisely the same powers of manifestation. After all, in the truest sense of the word, you are the same as your originating Spirit—the separate sense of self that Troward refers to comes from that troublesome ego.

To understand the power of contemplation, you must strive to understand the law of your being as one that allows you to use your thought processes to remain aligned with Spirit or Source energy.

While I recognize that the information in this section may seem a bit too esoteric for your tastes, if you carefully digest the works of Thomas Troward—and the creative process in you as a self-actualizing individual—you'll clearly see that contemplation is a powerful tool that may have escaped you up until now. That's because of your focus on your ego and the excuses you've employed to explain away your deficiencies.

Try imagining that everything and everyone originates in formless energy that you agree to call "Spirit," and then envision Spirit as a creative force that uses contemplation to express itself in a material form. You are an individualized expression of that same contemplation, so you have the possibility of doing precisely the same thing. The only requirement is that you don't dismiss your spiritual nature and replace it with a false self. The false self contemplates from a position of excuses, because it cannot manifest the creative energy necessary for the life it desires.

The mechanics of contemplation boil down to this:

- Contemplation is the *continual* use of your thought process.

- Your thoughts are actually like things that act to begin the process of materialization.

- If you contemplate with thoughts that *match* originating Spirit, you have the same power as originating Spirit.

- When contemplation is a vibrational match to originating Spirit, you gain the cooperation of Divine mind, attracting and fulfilling your desires.

- Contemplation is therefore a kind of action in and of itself, which sets into motion all of the creative forces of the universe.

- When you rely on excuses, you allow your false self (ego) to concentrate on what you *don't* want or why you can't create it for yourself.

- The presence of excuses in your life is evidence that you focus on what you can't do or have, rather than the infinite possibilities that are inherent in your Divine creative self.

- To rid yourself of excuses, you must learn to practice contemplating what you intend to manifest, and simultaneously detach from the outcome.

- Contemplate like God does, with thoughts of *How may I serve?* rather than *What's in it for me?*

- Remember Troward's famous observation: "The law of floatation was not discovered by contemplating the sinking of things . . ." In other words, when you see what you contemplate as if it's already here, the universe will ultimately offer you experiences that match what you're contemplating.

Suggestions for Implementing a New Way of Contemplating

— Thomas Troward urges us to grasp the idea that the contemplation of Spirit as power is the way for the individual to generate that same power within him- or herself. "We all have it in us," he says, and "it depends upon us to get it out into expression."

Your mind is always contemplating something, mulling this or that over and over again. Take some time each day (or even several times each day) to contemplate Spirit as power, rather than continuing the inner dialogue that generally results in your latching on to the same old excuse patterns. Try something like this: *The creative and intelligent power manifests perfectly as the universe. I am a result of this power. I feel connected to it, and I know it will work with me in creating the life I desire.* See your mind as a powerful force that's in harmony with the same power that's behind all of creation. Contemplate just this one idea, and you'll activate an *Excuses Begone!* cosmology for yourself.

— Begin the practice of viewing contemplation as action, rather than as passive mental meandering. Treasure your mind as a grand gift from your Creator, a gift so wondrous that it has the Creator's mind inside of it as well. View your contemplative moments the same way you view your practice time for improving your skills at any endeavor. An hour a day throwing a bowling ball is action that leads to a higher bowling average; a few moments several times a day musing about what you intend to manifest in some area of your life will have precisely the same effect on your *manifesting* average. Contemplation is action. It's necessary mind training for the implementation of anything you desire.

— Repeat the following mantra to yourself for a minimum of five straight minutes each day: *I contemplate myself surrounded by the conditions I wish to attract into my life.* Say it quickly and repeatedly, even if it sounds ludicrous to do so. The repetition will help you begin to imagine the right people or circumstances, the necessary funding, or whatever it is you desire. Stay detached and allow the universe to take care of the details. Stop focusing on those ancient excuses of yours and instead cooperate with the all-creating universal mind that can do anything and is part and parcel of your Divine self.

— I'm closing this chapter with one of Thomas Troward's pieces of advice, which has served me flawlessly since I was first made aware of his contribution to the art of mental science. This is the practice I've employed in manifesting my own desires for several decades now. Allow Troward's words on manifesting your heart's desire to resonate with you, even if his wording may appear to be convoluted and unusual:

> Simply [use] the one method of Creative Process, that is, the self-contemplation of Spirit. We now know ourselves to be Reciprocals of the Divine Spirit, centers in which It finds a fresh standpoint for Self-contemplation; and so the way to rise to the heights of this Great Pattern is by contemplating [and/or appreciating] it as the Normal Standard of our own Personality [individuality].

Allow yourself to reflect upon the above paragraph until it registers. You gain the power of creation by contemplating yourself as you are already!

CHAPTER 8

THE FIFTH PRINCIPLE: WILLINGNESS

*"If you are willing to be lived by it, you will see
it everywhere, even in the most ordinary things."*

— Lao-tzu

The word *willingness* describes a sizable concept. You might immediately think, *Of course I'm willing . . . willing to think or do anything at all in order to live a life of success, happiness, and super health.* Yet my experience as a helping professional for more than 40 years—as well as my being a man who attempts to help himself live what he writes about—has led me to a different conclusion. Most of us actually just give lip service to a life of higher awareness; we don't always want to undertake the necessary steps to create the life we desire. For this reason I've chosen to explore with you the fifth *Excuses Begone!* principle: willingness, an essential element in the approach toward living your life fully.

Four Key Questions about Willingness

Habituated thinking is largely the result of the memes you've allowed into your brain. The sole function of these mind viruses is to make umpteen copies of themselves and then infiltrate and spread wherever possible. While you might have been unaware that you were able to choose to reject those memes, the choice was nevertheless available. Although it may have been very difficult for you to overcome early influences—perhaps you believed it to be way too burdensome and exhausting an undertaking—you were still unwilling to do so.

Right now, declare yourself on the side of willingness rather then unwillingness. Begin in this present moment to kick those old excuse patterns down the stairs, one step at a time.

Ask yourself the following four questions, which will reinforce your willingness thoughts:

1. Am I Willing to Take Total Responsibility for All of the Conditions of My Life?

Examine how much you fault other people and circumstances for keeping you from achieving the level of success, happiness, and health you'd like to be enjoying—are you willing to stop doing this? Blaming others for deficiencies or any of the conditions of your life keeps you from fulfilling your own highest destiny.

Everyone in life does exactly what they know how to do given the conditions of their lives. That's the way I've chosen to look at the factors that made up the story of my life. For example, my mother had three small children under the age of four; and an alcoholic, thieving husband who walked away without ever providing any support. She placed one of my brothers and me in a series of foster homes, while my other brother lived with my grandmother until I was ten years old. This is not a story of pity or blame; it's precisely what had to take place in order for me to learn about self-reliance firsthand. Because I've lived self-reliance, and then gone on to teach it to millions of people, I don't find fault with anyone for any of the conditions of my life.

I see all of my early-childhood experiences as necessary gifts, even the ones laced with pain and sadness. Of course my past wasn't all roses, but then again, *no one's* past is all roses. There are times when life presents challenges, when good fortune turns into bad, when your roses die . . . that's just the way things go. There's no need for blame, since that only serves to provide a host of excuses.

Be willing to accept total responsibility for every facet of your own life. You didn't inherit your personality traits from anyone in your past—you've repeatedly chosen them, even though you may be unaware of how or why. If you're shy, loud, fearful, assertive, loving, hateful, kind, cruel, passive, or aggressive, learn to assert: *This is what I have chosen for myself up until now.* Similarly, if you find yourself mired in debt, languishing in poverty, wasting away in an unfulfilling career, wilting in an unsatisfying partnership, in pain over someone's poor business decisions, or even bored out of your mind because your parents made you pursue a career not of your liking—whatever the current conditions of your life, ask yourself if you're willing to take sole and total responsibility for them.

Begin by focusing on the following subjects:

— **The current status of your body.** Are you overweight, out of shape, plagued by annoying discomforts, constantly fatigued, or susceptible to many disease patterns from the polluted environment you live in? You do yourself a huge disservice if you're unwilling to say, with conviction, "In some way that I don't fully understand, I've made myself a vibrational match to all of the conditions of my life, and I'm willing to take all of the responsibility for these conditions. It's no one's fault; I bear full responsibility."

— **All that you are, all that you have (or don't have), and all that has come your way.** Yes, it's easier to cast blame someplace else. But when you choose an *Excuses Begone!* life, you put the steering wheel of your life back in your hands where it belongs. I'm aware that taking responsibility often appears difficult—accidents, mistreatment, abandonment, and dreary circumstances can certainly make life challenging. Being willing doesn't mean feeling a sense of personal shame or guilt over wrongdoings that may have been perpetrated upon you, nor does it mean believing that you've been punished because of some karmic payback. You indeed may have suffered at the hands of uneducated, poorly informed, badly addicted people. It was *not* your fault.

Even as we recognize this, I still urge you to accept, without guilt, that everything that has shown up in your life has value equal to your assuming responsibility for its existence. At the very least, be willing to accept it as you would an unwanted, uninvited child whom you've come to care for through unforeseen circumstances.

There's something for you to learn in any difficulty. Be willing to say, "Thank You, God, for the experiences I've lived through" on a daily basis. Look for the blessing in all situations, and remind yourself that you're no longer a child, but a fully functioning adult who's ready to accept responsibility.

In the 1st century A.D., slave-turned-philosopher Epictetus offered this wisdom: "It is the act of an ill-instructed man to blame others for his own bad condition; it is the act of one who has begun to be instructed, to lay the blame on himself; and of one whose instruction is completed, neither to blame another, nor himself."

Your own instruction can be completed by successfully following an *Excuses Begone!* way of life. Blame must be supplanted by a willingness to look at everything that occurs in your life and choosing to think, *I attracted and created it all, and I am happy to take full and sole responsibility for all of it.* As an ancient Hindu proverb reminds us: "He who cannot dance claims the floor is uneven." If you can't dance, that's your choice. But if you want to get out there and enjoy yourself, there's nothing holding you back . . . except your excuses.

2. Am I Willing to Surrender?

Ridding yourself of excuses involves receptivity to turning yourself over to something greater than your own little ego. In order to live the life that's waiting to materialize for you, you simply must be willing to let go of the one you may have been planning for years. As Lao-tzu puts it so succinctly: "If you want to be given everything, give everything up." While it may sound strange to you now, the thing you surrender to becomes your power.

In the first question in this section, you asked yourself if you were willing to take full responsibility for all of the conditions of your life. Now you must discover whether you're able to let go to the point that it becomes almost second nature. By surrendering to a higher power, you become intimately familiar with the highest place within you: your true, infinite, co-creating self.

If you're immersed in the workings of the ego, you may not even have the faintest idea of what is meant by subordinating yourself to a higher principle. If this is the case for you, then your false self is the beginning and the end, the sum of all your existence. Abandoning excuses is not a likely outcome in that scenario, so simply recite this sentence to yourself: "I'm willing to surrender to that all-creating force responsible for all of life coming into form, and to allow myself to be lived by it, rather than my living it."

I love the words of Ramana Maharshi, who sees this subject as applying not to some external higher being, but rather to the highest part of yourself: "Surrender is giving oneself up to the original cause of one's being. Do not delude yourself by imagining this source to be some God outside you. One's source is within oneself. Give yourself up to it."

The secret is to let yourself be lived by that highest part of yourself. As Lao-tzu's observation at the beginning of this chapter states: "If you are willing to be lived by it, you will see it everywhere, even in the most ordinary things." While the pesky ego keeps telling you to run the show, that wise spiritual teacher from ancient China and I encourage you to do the reverse. Why not give in to this notion and let yourself be lived by the creative spirit that is always within you? Just let go . . . recognize that you own nothing, that you're doing nothing, and that it is all being done right before your eyes. Surrender and become less attached to the ego-dominated idea that the world is giving you a raw deal. This *is* the deal, period.

You came here when you were supposed to, and you will leave on time, independent of your opinion about it. If you watch your body aging, you know that you aren't making the changes to it—they're just being made. Your body is being lived by the great Tao, the all-creating Source. If your ego were truly in charge, you would never wrinkle, see age spots, get gray hair, or die. Like it or not, something greater than ego is in charge of everything.

Now extend this same thinking to all of your life, beyond your body, and release yourself to this great energy source. As my teacher Nisargadatta Maharaj once put it: "Spiritual maturity lies in the readiness to let go of everything. The giving up is the first step. But the real giving up is in realizing that there is nothing to give up, for nothing is your own." As hard as it may be for you to realize, when you relinquish, you produce riches. Willingness to surrender means never needing excuses again. In the end, it's all just the way it is. God doesn't need excuses—and since you and God are one, you don't need them either.

3. Am I Willing to Hold the Vision?

It's one thing to make a pronouncement in a moment of inspiration about what you intend to manifest in your life or what kind of a person you intend to become. It's quite another to make a commitment to holding that vision regardless of what difficulties or obstacles may surface. Holding the vision involves an unwillingness to compromise what you're visualizing for yourself.

It means being willing to suffer through criticism and what appears to be an uncooperative universe.

To get to this level, you have to be willing to release some mighty powerful images that you've carried with you since you were a young child . . . images that are very likely entrenched in that 18-item excuse catalog I wrote about in Chapter 3. Excuses aren't just words explaining the lack of success in various areas of your life—they also show up as pictures or visions that you carry around with you, a series of photos that you see projected on your inner screen.

These visuals are strong because they've appeared on your screen so many times in so many varied circumstances that they've become reality. Even though they're excuse-based images that define your imagined self with all of its shortcomings, they've become your guides. They've stood the test of time and have been reinforced by many well-meaning friends and family members. They're like trusted confidants, giving you the same advice and encouragement about dealing with life from a perspective of what you can't accomplish, how unlucky you are, or how unfortunate you are to have the life experiences you've had. They're quite adept at showing you how to compromise and settle for less than you might have hoped for.

Your old pictures don't fade or disintegrate quickly, and the screen they appear on can't seem to display anything else. These images of your destiny have ultimately become the definition of you—you've looked at them for so long and become so accustomed to them that you've forgotten that they're actually false. So if you see yourself as undeserving of financial success, you act on that "unworthy" image. The fact that this is a mind virus caught from many other minds is of no consequence. It's still defining *your* reality and hindering *you* from projecting alternative pictures for yourself.

You can readjust your willingness meter to avow that you're open to seeing an alternative vision by affirming: *I am worthy of attracting unlimited abundance and prosperity into my life, regardless of what life experiences have gone before me. I only reinforce and contemplate images that are in harmony with this vision.* After all, it's your inner screen and yours alone. No one from your past has exclusive rights to what plays on your screen—you can display whatever you deem appropriate and can delete anything you choose.

Now let's go back to the third question in this section. Even if you're not convinced that you can change or make something happen that has never happened before, are you in fact willing to hold a new vision? If your response isn't a wholehearted "Yes!" see if there's an old picture on your inner screen; if so, allow it to disintegrate as you watch. Eventually, you'll be willing to hold the vision of yourself as smart, energetic, and deserving of the best that life has to offer. When that happens, you'll be a vibrational match to the Source of all, and this new receptivity will become your *Excuses Begone!* way of life.

As the Bible warns: "Where there is no vision, the people perish" (Proverbs 29:18). I'd add that when you have a *faulty* vision based on excuses and memes, you'll also perish. Not in the literal sense of course—but if you insist on remaining a being who's living an unfulfilled life, then the authentic you destined for greatness, happiness, success, and health will die.

Hold a vision that asserts: "I'm entitled to be respected, loved, and happy; to feel fulfilled and prosperous; to exercise; and to enjoy all the moments of my life! This is my vision, and I'm more than willing—I'm absolutely *determined* that this is what will come my way." When anything crops up that's inconsistent with this vision, take the advice of Lao-tzu: "In order to eliminate the negative influences, simply ignore them." Such words are so simple, yet so profound.

4. Am I Willing to Shed All Unwillingness?

The concept of unwillingness might be even more significant than willingness when it comes to adopting the *Excuses Begone!* way. So what are *you* reluctant to do in order to make your dreams and desires become your reality?

Are you unwilling to change locations and move to another city? To leave your parents or your grown children in order to start a life that you've dreamed about? To quit your current job because of all the benefits you'd lose? To end a long-term relationship that you know is wrong for you because of the discomfort it would cause in others? To spend the money that you've saved for emergencies to invest in a dream of your own today? To overcome your fear of beginning a new exercise regimen that you know would benefit you? To enroll in a college course because you feel that you're too old to learn something new? To get the help you need to overcome an addiction that continues to wreak havoc in your life? To stand up to family members or co-workers who continue to treat you unfairly? As you can see, this list of examples could go on forever.

Develop your own list of things you're unwilling to do in order to re-create your life. Then find a big eraser and rub out those excuses on your list. After adding the header ALL THE THINGS I'M UNWILLING TO DO IN ORDER TO LIVE THE LIFE THAT I INTEND TO LIVE—THE LIFE I SIGNED UP FOR EVEN BEFORE I CAME INTO THIS BODY IN THIS WORLD, keep this smudged and perhaps tattered sheet of paper in a prominent place. Use it as your reminder to erase the concept of unwillingness from your consciousness.

In 1975 when I'd written my first book for public consumption, I recall my agent Artie Pine asking me, "Is there anything that you're unwilling to do in order to create the kind of excitement in the country that will make this book a big success?" The answer was no, I was willing to do anything: pay my own expenses; travel the entire country; stay up all night, night after night, talking on call-in radio; do 12 to 14 interviews a day; take my family with me on this adventure; and buy up the first two printings of the book to distribute myself. All the while, I was having the time of my life living what I considered to be my purpose, telling anyone who would listen about the commonsense ideas that filled the pages of *Your Erroneous Zones*.

Similarly, when I first began to record lectures for public television, I made up my mind that there would be nothing on my unwillingness list. I visited more than 170 TV stations to talk about the ideas and raise money for PBS throughout the country—there were no stations too small for me to visit. I was willing to do this for seven days a week during entire pledge periods, flying from city to city, staying up late and getting up in the middle of the night to go on to the next place, most of the time paying my own expenses, yet always living my passion.

And even though I'm now in my 68th year, I still have nothing on my unwillingness list. When it comes to my film, *The Shift*, I love it so much that nothing will hold me back from telling the world about it. I know that if enough people view it, it's capable of changing not only individual lives, but the entire planet as well.

The payoffs for having a blank unwillingness sheet are monumental. The biggest and most basic one is that you have no excuses to fall back on when you're explaining what's missing in your life; there's nothing to find fault with and no one to blame. You simply do whatever you need to do to fulfill your dreams, and you have the luxury of not needing to explain your actions to anyone. (You may want to include some items on your own list such as being unwilling to lie, steal, cheat, be immoral, break the law, and so on. I didn't write about these because I'm assuming that such behaviors are inconsistent with who you are as a being aligned with your Source.)

Now let me ask you this: what is it that you've been loath to think or do in order to create the life that you're desirous of living? Anything that crops up in your mind is likely to be in that catalog from Chapter 3. *It would have taken too long, so I didn't sign up for the training. It would have caused too much of a disruption to my family, so I didn't follow my intuition. I'm too old to make such changes, so I was unwilling to begin an entirely new endeavor. The money wasn't there, and I couldn't justify the expense at the time.* These and many more like them sound like legitimate reasons for not fulfilling that inner calling that your heart knows is your true dharma, your ultimate purpose.

There's nothing rational about what I'm asking you to consider here, nor is this an intellectual exercise I'm imploring you to contemplate—this is your *heart* I'm speaking to, not your head. When you feel that there's something for you to do, and that inner voice will not be silenced, I urge you to look at that sheet of paper that represents what you will not do to fulfill your destiny. By all means, stay aligned with your Source and live from a God-realized perspective, but remind yourself, *There's nothing I'm unwilling to think or do (as long as it is aligned with my Source) in order to bring my dreams into reality.* When you discard unwillingness from your life, you'll be guided to a place where any and all excuses will definitely be . . . gone!

Suggestions for Applying a
Willingness Mind-set to Your Life

— End the blame game once and for all. Begin to see all of your personal traits and the conditions you experience as choices rather than factors that came about because of some external circumstances. Refer to everything in your life with statements such as, "I chose to listen to what my parents said when I was a child, and I'm still under their influence in some ways today," rather than "I can't help the way I am; I've always been this way, and it's largely the fault of my early training." Similarly, state: "I've always been fearful about leaving this job or city because I've made other people's opinions more important than my own," rather than "I can't help being fearful—I was trained by my parents, who have always been afraid to try something new themselves."

Be willing to say these words and mean them: "I'm the product of all of the choices I've made in my life. I have no one to blame for anything that isn't going the way I'd like it to go, including myself."

— Practice being willing to hold the vision by rehearsing scenes in your mind that deal with others who aren't in agreement with your new stance. Don't argue with family members or partners who think you're foolish to have a vision for yourself that's incompatible with the one they have of you. Instead, simply respond with, "Thank you for sharing your vision; your opinions are always helpful to me." And then—and this is important—*hold on to your vision even tighter* and make every effort to act on it without being confrontational.

If you're determined to get a college degree or complete some kind of specialized training that you've always wanted, and others around you think that such ambitions are preposterous, silently note: *What you think of me is none of my business.* Then hold the vision. Your vision of yourself and your willingness to hold on to it through resistance from others is crucial to your *Excuses Begone!* life.

— Create an inventory of the things you're unwilling to do in order to manifest your destiny. Then erase everything on it but this title: WHAT I AM UNWILLING TO THINK OR DO IN ORDER TO BECOME ALL THAT I DESIRE FOR MYSELF. Leave this sheet of paper in a prominent spot, where you can look at it every day to remind you of your commitment to shed all unwillingness. When you're challenged and find yourself reverting to old habits, look at your empty sheet, and then affirm the following for at least five minutes: *There is nothing that I am unwilling to think or do in order to become all that I am destined to become.* Repeating this inner mantra will serve as an energy shifter for you, and it will put you on the path of greatness.

Virginia Woolf once offered a single line that has guided me throughout my adult life: "Arrange whatever pieces come your way." I pass it along to you with this caveat: you must be willing to take whatever pieces of life come your way and arrange them so that they work *with* and *for* you rather than *against* you. The key is to be willing. The pieces will show up—they always have, and they always will. Your willingness to arrange rather than complain or make excuses will pay off.

CHAPTER 9

THE SIXTH PRINCIPLE: *PASSION*

"When a man's willing and eager, God joins in."

— Aeschylus

Memorize these four words: *passion always trumps excuses!* However, keep in mind that when I use the word *passion,* I'm not referring to the romantic notions that this concept conjures. Instead, I'm equating it to a vigorous kind of enthusiasm that you feel deep within you and that isn't easy to explain or define. This kind of passion propels you in a direction that seems motivated by a force beyond your control. It's the inner excitement of being on the right path, doing what feels good to you and what you know you were meant to do.

It's my contention that the mere *presence* of passion within you—and the enthusiasm that comes with it—is all you need to fulfill your dreams. And let's take a brief look at the word *enthusiasm.* As the novelist and woman of letters Madame de Staël noted in 1810: "The sense of this word among the Greeks affords the noblest definition of it; enthusiasm signifies God in us."

Earlier I wrote that God is in no need of excuses, ever. The creative Divine Spirit is able to manifest anything it contemplates, and you and I are the results of its contemplating itself into material form. Thus, when we have an emotional reaction that feels like overwhelming passion for what *we're* contemplating, we're experiencing the God within us . . . and nothing can hold us back. Enthusiasm becomes our co-creator.

I take you back to those four words that I opened this chapter with: *passion always trumps excuses.* Stay with your passion, and excuses will most assuredly be . . . gone!

Enthusiasm Overcomes Excuses

Passion is a feeling that tells you: *This is the right thing to do. Nothing can stand in my way. It doesn't matter what anyone else says. This feeling is so good that it cannot be ignored. I'm going to follow my bliss and act upon this glorious sensation of joy.*

Excuses, on the other hand, communicate the opposite message: *I don't necessarily have to follow through—look at how dull all of this is anyway. This isn't very important; if it was, I'd be excited about it. I'll drop it for now; I can always do it later. This isn't really for me; I'll just finish it quickly and get it over with.*

Think of Madame de Staël's definition of *enthusiasm,* that it signifies God in you. If you can imagine God at work creating beingness (form) out of nonbeingness (Spirit), you'll begin to understand the assertion of Jesus that "with God all things are possible." So if all things are possible with God, and God is within you in the form of your passionate enthusiasm, why would you ever need to employ an excuse of any kind?

When you're enthusiastic, nothing seems difficult. When you have passion, there are no risks: family dramas become meaningless, money isn't an issue, you know that you have the strength and the smarts, and the rules laid down by others have no bearing on you whatsoever. That's because you're answering your calling— and the you who is doing the answering is the highest part of you, or the God within.

The presence of passion within you is the greatest gift you can receive. And when it's aligned with Spirit, treat it as a miracle, doing everything you can to hold on to it. I feel this way about the creation of my books. I've learned over the years that when I go to that place of passion within me, there's no force in the universe that can interfere with my completing a project. I live and breathe it, keeping notepads close at hand when I eat, drive, practice yoga, and even sleep. My life is consumed by the passion I feel for what I'm doing—yet I know that as long as I feel this, I'm experiencing the God within.

My enthusiasm seems to cause my world to endlessly offer me cooperative, co-creating experiences. Ideas come to me in my sleep, and I awaken and jot them down. Ideas flow to me in yoga class, and I make a mental note to record them when I've finished exercising. I'm willing and I'm eager, and not just about my writing—I feel the same way about staying in shape, enjoying my family, preparing to do a film, giving a lecture, or whatever it may be. As the famed Greek dramatist Aeschylus suggested in the quote that opens this chapter, when willingness and eagerness are present, "God joins in." This is why I say that the presence of passion is so critical. It doesn't just help us emulate the all-creating Divine mind; it allows us to become one with it again.

If you have passion, there is no need for excuses, because your enthusiasm will trump any reasoning you might come up with. Your excitement will propel you toward acting on what you've been imagining with such gusto that you won't need an explanation for what is holding you back. While this doesn't guarantee that your venture will be financially successful or well received, it *does* guarantee that you'll follow it through to completion, since the force behind it is God within you.

Enthusiasm makes excuses a nonissue. When you seek the presence of your creative Spirit and are filled with passion about virtually everything you undertake, you'll successfully remove the roadblocks from your life and enjoy the active presence of Spirit.

Activating Passion in Your Life

Comfort and luxury are usually the chief requirements of life for your ego—its top priorities tend to be accumulations, achievements, and the approval of others. Consider a new alternative for what makes you happy, one that soars beyond the superficial demands of the ego. The only thing that you need for this state of joy is something to be passionate about. Something that speaks only to you . . . that gets you tingling inside with excitement . . . that will not go away . . . that radiates within you . . . that sends you into a frenzy of good feeling because it makes you feel purposeful and connected to your Source of being. It doesn't matter what it is. The only requirement is that you feel intensely about it and are willing to act with enthusiasm, awakening the sleeping God within you.

As Abraham Maslow once observed about self-actualizing people: "They must be what they can be." Take a moment now to think about what you can be, and contrast that with what you've chosen to be up until now. So what *can* you be? You might decide to become passionate about getting yourself in optimal physical shape. Are you able to walk up a few flights of stairs without gasping for air? Are you capable of running ten miles without being totally exhausted? Are you carrying excessive weight? Are you in that high percentage of people who fall into the obesity range? Do you treat your body as a temple, attending to its highest needs? Can you become zealous about living a healthy life?

Perhaps you have an idea that you've been carrying around with you for decades, such as a book that you know needs to be written, which only *you* have the wisdom to create. Can you get so passionate about realizing your vision that you activate the presence of God to assist you in co-creating your dreams? Remember, the mere presence of that passion, nothing more, is evidence that the energy of the Divine creating spirit is alive and well in you. That's all you need—just the willingness to allow your passion to speak up and awaken from its dormant status. You don't have to know *how* to activate your long-buried enthusiasm or precisely *what* to focus on. What you need is the willingness to say yes to signals from within you, the God within you who wants to be active.

I've always treasured the observations of the famous Greek scholar Nikos Kazantzakis, who is one of my favorite authors. In page after page of his wonderful novel *Zorba the Greek*, Kazantzakis details what a truly passionate man looks, sounds, and feels like, as the title character simply lives his bliss and feels the presence of God in every waking moment. And I've had these words by Kazantzakis posted in my home for more than a decade now, yet I still read and contemplate them every day: "By believing passionately in something that does not yet exist we create it. The nonexistent is whatever we have not sufficiently desired." The "something that does not yet exist" for you has very likely been explained away repeatedly with any number of excuses, and what's "not sufficiently desired" describes the absence of passion to a tee.

Returning for a moment to the ideas I brought up in the last chapter, practice both holding the vision for your life and surrendering it to a power greater than yourself—one that you're also connected to at all times. As I always respond whenever I'm asked what my secret is for having overcome a mountain of various addictions in my life: "I turned the entire matter over to a higher power, and I began to passionately believe in something that did not yet exist." I've come to see passion as synonymous with God. When I began to fervently hold on to my vision for myself, I accessed the Divine guidance that steered my life away from harmful substances and behaviors: suddenly I'd find new circumstances that were addiction free, the right people started showing up, and the wrong people became "mysteriously" unable to contact me.

Give this new enthusiastic vision a try. Believe in its ability to not only kindle the fire inside of you, but keep it alive as well. Draw it, smell it, sense it, smile about it, and see it coming to you on the wings of angels right into your life. Let go of those tedious, worn-out justifications for what you haven't been able to produce, and take comfort in Zorba's model of a passionate person. Begin to believe in the nonexistent you rather than in a part of you that's stuck in place and full of excuses. Get excited about your vision and know that when you change the way you look at things, the things you look at change. Revisit passion within yourself and see how the world not only looks different, but acts differently *toward* you.

Enthusiasm Is Inspiring

Enthusiasm enables you to stay "in-Spirit" or inspired. And just like anything else (including excuses), the more you access and hold on to enthusiasm, the more it becomes a habit. The best thing about this particular habit, however, is that it's always accompanied by joy and happiness. To that end, James Baldwin once wrote that "fires can't be made with dead embers, nor can enthusiasm be stirred by spiritless men."

The best way to keep your passion alive is to make your number one relationship in the world be that between you and your Source of being. Stay in a state of wonderment and bewilderment over everything and everyone you encounter. Go through life being continuously grateful and appreciative—give thanks for all of nature and the multitude of miracles you see appearing before your eyes each and every day. This is a daily practice for me, and it's the most prominent factor I can identify for keeping my zest for life alive and well.

I'm in awe of this entire business that we call life. I sit here writing, yet not having a clue about how it all takes place. Words appear on the page from *no where* and suddenly they are *now here*. Where did they come from? Is someone guiding me? And what about those trees outside my window, or that tiny little creature crawling across the page of the book I just opened, which have the same life force in them that I have in me? And those stars and galaxies out there . . . are we alone in this vast, endless universe?

I could go on and on writing about the gazillion things there are to be passionate about. The point is that there's no shortage of things to inspire us. And by staying in this space of wonderment, bewilderment, and especially gratitude, we feel the excitement of being alive. This is a far different stance from the one that exists when we rely on excuses to explain our life's deficiencies away.

The longer I live, the more I'm content to allow unseen powers work their magic with and around me, and the less I question any of it. I have relinquished the notion that I'm ever separate from the all-knowing mind of the universe. In this state of awe, I feel passion all the time. I don't need to do anything—I feel it in every face I look into and in every star-filled night and blossoming flower I observe. My greatest moments of enthusiasm occur while trying to think and act like the all-knowing, benevolent Source of everything does; when I let go of ego, I'm most able to maintain my passion.

Lao-tzu once observed: "If your willingness to give blessings is limited, so also is your ability to receive them. This is the subtle operation of the Tao." Your own willingness to give blessings can be totally unrestricted. By staying aligned with the way the all-creating Tao works, you maintain an exceptionally high level of enthusiasm, and it all seems to make so much sense. When you stay aligned with God and think like God thinks, you act as God seems to act. You live in-Spirit—and with enthusiasm.

Nurturing Your Passion

Experiencing that thrill of passion in your body is an indication that you're fulfilling a destiny you may have signed up for even before you merged into the world of being from nonbeing. The opening lines of the Old Testament convey that "God" and "good" are essentially synonymous, so know that when you feel good, that's akin to saying that you feel *God*.

The presence of passion (feeling good) is also the same as having God awakened within yourself. Think of this awakened presence as something you need to continuously pay attention to and nurture in order to prevent it from either going back to sleep or disappearing entirely. In other words, you must keep this passion ever-present on the front burner of your life.

I encourage you to spend as much energy as you can reaching out and helping other people. Recall Lao-tzu's message that your willingness to *receive* blessings is related to your ability to *give* them. I know that I feel the greatest passion when I'm in the process of serving others. Giving money to individuals to finance dreams that otherwise would go unfulfilled or sending books and CDs to hospitals, prisons, libraries, and schools is always a thrill for me. Even taking my 92-year-old mom out for dinner, just the two of us, sends waves of pleasure down my spine.

Giving to others is a great first step in finding your passion. Recently, for instance, I had the opportunity to spend a morning in a first-grade classroom (I was invited to read *Unstoppable Me!* one of the four children's books I've co-authored with Kristina Tracy). Interacting with the children and hearing the questions they asked filled me with enthusiasm, but what I saw in their teacher, Ms. Wimmer, was equally thrilling. Here's a woman living her passion every day through serving those first graders—she radiates her joy in nurturing the love of learning in all of her students, and she glows with excitement as she talks about each of the boys and girls whom she feels honored to teach.

Her students simply adore this wonderful educator, and who can blame them? She takes them on after-school field trips, has them write their own illustrated books, plans elaborate graduation ceremonies, and gets down on the floor with them to instruct from a hands-on perspective. Every subject is taught from a creative point of view.

Ms. Wimmer is also more than willing to spend her own money to provide experiences for the kids in her classroom who wouldn't otherwise have the opportunity due to budgetary considerations. There simply are no limits to what she'll do to give her students an ideal first-grade experience. This is passionate nurturing!

Rather than using our days to just go through the motions and feel a sense of ennui, we all need to go through life as enthusiastically as Ms. Wimmer does. After all, how can we be expected to find any passion if we're seemingly stuck in a dull world that typifies our daily existence? We must discover the joy and satisfaction that comes from feeding our passion—it's a much better idea than hauling out that tiresome excuse that "life is boring."

It may be helpful to think of your passion as the presence of the creative Source inside you. Talk to this invisible yet tangible presence within and thank it for never abandoning you. Go for walks with it and even imagine holding hands with it. Ask it questions and listen to what it has to say, making mental notes of how it is directing you. Feel enormous gratitude for the reality of this presence, and allow it to guide you in any way it wishes.

Always remember that your passion is evidence of God within, and you can make it your own very private experience. You don't need to share your inner stirring with anyone you feel might rain on your parade. Rather, make a promise to yourself that you'll pay attention to your passion, that you'll do at least one small thing daily to make it your reality. Even if you only do a silent meditation on keeping your dream alive, write one paragraph of the book you've been envisioning, make one phone call exploring how to get into that business you've fantasized about running, or put a few dollars aside to finance your future endeavor, do it. Pay attention to your passion—*never ignore it*. Talk to it so that you don't have to drag out excuses to explain why it was always impossible for you to see and follow your own bliss.

Keep in mind that your passion must be fed in order to survive; it will never let you down if you nurture it. How could it? It is God within you. And with God all things are possible . . . and no excuses are necessary.

Suggestions for Living a Passion-Filled Life

— Do something every day to keep the awakened God within from falling back asleep. Remember that your feelings of excitement are the result of the way you think, and when your thoughts harmonize with Source energy, you begin to feel your passion. Therefore, you must keep a constant watch on your mental activity. Maintain a journal to record what fires you up—the more you write, the more you invite passion to live within you.

Go on the Internet and view sites that talk about and promote ideas you feel enthusiastic about. Telephone or e-mail someone out there who shares the same vision as you. Open a private bank account that contains seed money to fund a passion. Whatever you do, remind yourself that this is *your passion* and you're feeding and nurturing it every day. As this becomes your habituated way of being, you'll see the universe cooperating and offering experiences that match your desires.

— Develop a sense of awe that then leads to the creation of passion by beginning to look at everything as though you're seeing it for the first time. Don't let the concept of boredom even creep into your thoughts.

I've participated in thousands of interviews of all types over the past four decades. Frequently I've been asked, "Don't you find it boring to be asked the same questions over and over?" My response, which comes from my heart, is: "I've never been interviewed by this person, at this time, on this subject, under these circumstances before." Thus, every interview is a brand-new joyful endeavor, and this keeps my passion alive. I employ the same kind of thinking when I'm about to give a lecture for the tenth time in two weeks—each presentation before a live audience is a novel experience.

Look at your entire life in this way: Make love to your spouse like it's the first time. Read to your children like it's the first time. Go for your daily run like it's the first time. Every new moment is a gift from the all-knowing Tao, so when you act as if each experience and moment is a fresh one, you'll feel the passion I'm attempting to convey in this book.

— Take a five-minute time-out today to repeat the following affirmation: *I invite the presence of God to be with me in the form of my passion.* This reminds you that every moment of excitement you feel is evidence that you have Divine guidance in the moment. By holding on to it, you'll enter the *Excuses Begone!* zone.

As Thomas Aquinas observed: "True peace consists in not separating ourselves from the will of God." All of your moments of excitement, enthusiasm, and passion are moments of connection. They bring true peace. Excuses, on the other hand, are what you employ when you separate yourself from your passion, or the will of God. Excuses are lifelong thinking habits that take you away from peace. You always have the choice: passion, peace, and alignment with God; or excuses, excuses, and more excuses.

CHAPTER 10

THE SEVENTH PRINCIPLE: COMPASSION

"True compassion is more than flinging a coin to a beggar . . . it understands that an edifice which produces beggars needs restructuring."
— Martin Luther King, Jr.

There is a widely told story that speaks to the value of compassion. It seems that a woman who lived a Tao-centered life came upon a precious stone while sitting by the banks of a running stream in the mountains, and she placed this highly valued item in her bag.

The next day, a hungry traveler approached the woman and asked for something to eat. As she reached into her bag for a crust of bread, the traveler saw the precious stone and imagined how it would provide him with financial security for the remainder of his life. He asked the woman to give the treasure to him, and she did, along with some food. He left, ecstatic over his good fortune and the knowledge that he was now secure.

A few days later the traveler returned and handed back the stone to the wise woman. "I've been thinking," he told her. "Although

I know how valuable this is, I'm returning it to you in the hopes that you could give me something even more precious."

"What would that be?" the woman inquired.

"Please give me what you have within yourself that enabled you to give me that stone."

The woman in this story was living her life from a sacred place of compassion . . . which is the seventh and last principle for an *Excuses Begone!* life.

Compassion and Excuses

It is impossible to need excuses when the focus of life shifts to *How may I serve?* Thinking of others first—reaching out to them despite how it might inconvenience you—causes you to feel joy, which is what the hungry traveler was actually seeking. This gift of feeling good (or feeling God) within comes from serving and surrendering rather than asking and demanding.

There's no room for blame in your life as long as you live with kindness. And excuses, regardless of their form, are all about blame. Blaming your past. Blaming the economy. Blaming your perceived personal flaws. Blaming God. Blaming your parents. Blaming your children or your spouse. Blaming your DNA. There's no shortage of circumstances, people, and events to blame—and there's no shortage of blame itself.

When you shift to compassion, all blame disappears. So no matter what you may want for yourself, discover how you can want it more for someone else, and then make that shift. In that contemplative moment, compassion will eradicate finger-pointing and trump excuse making. And you'll begin to think like God thinks: serving, offering, giving, and loving freely.

The wise woman in the mountains who gave the precious stone to a stranger had no need to think about poverty or unhappiness, to hold a cynical view toward the greedy masses, or to explain the way she lived her life. Why? Because her ego was out of the picture, and love and service reigned supreme.

I've certainly found that when I remember to nurture kindness and courtesy, everything in my life seems to move toward more harmony and peace, to say nothing of how much better I feel when I'm giving rather than wanting.

I heard the Dalai Lama speak on compassion some years back, and the essence of his message contained these two points:

1. Compassion is the single most important quality that humanity needs to learn. This is the way to find happiness and health and to feel successful.

2. War and violence would become extinct in one generation if, beginning at the age of five, children were taught to meditate on compassion for an hour a week for the rest of their lives. Such is the power of a compassionate approach to life, which is truly thinking of others and living by the ancient Golden Rule.

The very second you feel yourself retreating to excuses, repeat the mantra *How may I serve?* Then act upon the answers you receive. You'll become aligned with the universal mind, which is always giving, and the bonus is that you'll notice the universe asking you back, "How may I serve *you?*" As your compassion for others flows back to you, remember the truth I've written about many times in this book: *You do not attract what you want; you attract what you are.* So make compassion be what you are.

Three Questions

For the past several years I've celebrated Father's Day in a way that reflects what this chapter is about: I give special gifts to my eight children, rather than receiving presents from them. Being a father is one of the greatest privileges that I've enjoyed for more than 40 years. I consider it an incredible honor as well as a sacred undertaking to parent my six beautiful girls and two handsome sons, so it's my wish to thank them for choosing me as their dad and for allowing me to play this glorious role in their lives.

I think of the responsibility of raising and supporting a child as an amazing gift, because to be able to fully support another human being is as close to being in a place of God realization as there is. After all, when God contemplates us into existence, doesn't He/She support us, and allow the free will to choose a compassionate existence?

This past Father's Day, my gift to my children was a copy of Leo Tolstoy's short story *Three Questions*. Tolstoy tells of a king who was certain that if he just knew the best time to act; the right people to listen to; and, above all, the most important thing to do at all times, he'd never fail in anything he might undertake.

So he proclaimed that he would bountifully reward anyone in his kingdom who would teach him the answers to these three questions. Many learned men came to see the king, but since they all responded differently—and he didn't agree with any of them—none of these men were rewarded. But the king still greatly desired to have his three questions answered, so he decided to consult a hermit who was widely renowned for his wisdom.

The reclusive old man received only common folk, so the king put on simple clothes, left his bodyguards, dismounted from his horse, and went to see him alone. When the disguised king reached the hermit, he asked him his three questions, but the elder fellow didn't answer. Noting that the hermit was very frail and attempting to dig some flower beds, the king took over, shoveling earth for hours. When he attempted his questions again, the hermit noticed a bearded man running out of the woods, holding his hands over a profusely bleeding wound in his abdomen.

The hermit and the king took the bearded man inside and tended to him. The next morning, the man asked the king to forgive him, even though the ruler was certain he'd never seen this individual before.

The injured man explained:

> You do not know me, but I know you. I am that enemy of yours who swore to revenge himself on you, because you executed his brother and seized his property. I knew you had gone

alone to see the hermit, and I resolved to kill you on your way back. But the day passed and you did not return. So I came out from my ambush to find you, and I came upon your bodyguards, and they recognized me, and wounded me. I escaped from them, but should have bled to death had you not dressed my wound. I wished to kill you, and you have saved my life. Now, if I live, and if you wish it, I will serve you as your most faithful slave, and will bid my sons do the same. Forgive me!

The king not only forgave him, but he also said that he'd send his servants and his own physician to attend to the man, and he promised to give him back the property that had been taken from him.

At that point, the king went outside and saw the hermit placing seeds in the beds he'd dug the day before. He decided to ask the old sage his three questions one final time, and was surprised when the elderly fellow responded that his queries had already been answered:

"How answered? What do you mean?" asked the king.

"Do you not see," replied the hermit. "If you had not pitied my weakness yesterday, and had not dug these beds for me, but had gone your way, that man would have attacked you, and you would have repented of not having stayed with me. So the most important time was when you were digging the beds; and I was the most important man; and to do me good was your most important business. Afterwards when that man ran to us, the most important time was when you were attending to him, for if you had not bound up his wounds he would have died without having made peace with you. So he was the most important man, and what you did for him was your most important business. Remember then: there is only one time that is important—Now! It is the most important time because it is the only time when we have any power. The most necessary man is he with whom you are, for no man knows whether he will ever have dealings with anyone else: and the most important affair is, to do him good, because for that purpose alone was man sent into this life!"

Let's go over the three questions as they pertain to your living from a place of compassion. As you read this section, think about the lessons that the king learned from his wise teacher, the hermit; as well as what can be taken from the example of the wise woman who gave away her precious stone to a traveler.

1. When Is the Best Time to Do Each Thing?

Both the hermit and the wise woman understood what Tolstoy meant when he wrote: "Remember then: there is only one time that is important—Now! It is the most important time because it is the only time when we have any power." You may recall that the third *Excuses Begone!* principle explained that compassion can only be experienced in this current moment. *Now* is where everything takes place. So your relationship to life is truly your relationship to the present.

I love the definition of compassion offered by historian Arnold Toynbee: "Compassion is the desire that moves the individual self to widen the scope of its self-concern to embrace the whole of the universal self."

In any given moment of your life, when you embrace another beyond any concern for yourself, you are living compassion . . . you're also making it impossible to employ excuses. Thus, you now know the secret that Tolstoy's king sought and the wise woman knew instinctively: *This is the time to widen your scope beyond self-concern and embrace a universal self that includes everyone, especially the person who is before you.*

Can you imagine that compassionate woman or wise hermit coming up with an excuse for life not working at the level they liked? Be like them and recognize that this moment is your power—seize it and extend compassion without regard for yourself. And remember that your appointment with life is always in the present.

2. Who Are the Most Important People to Work With?

We often hear about, and respond to, the importance of offering assistance to others in drastic need in faraway places. As we try to work toward bringing about world peace, we join organizations dedicated to improving the lives of those who are most needy. Yet this doesn't answer this second question adequately.

Whoever is in your immediate space is the most important person for you to work with, be it friend, family member, co-worker, or total stranger. Therefore, extend kindness to whomever you see before you. As Tolstoy reminds you, you can't know that you'll ever have dealings with anyone else. *This* is your moment, and the person to work with is right there. The wise woman understood this well—she wasn't saving the precious stone for herself, for someone more deserving, or for a relative. She gave her gift, which came from her compassionate heart, to a person she'd never met before. So the lesson is: Don't look beyond the moment. Now is a perfect opportunity. Whoever is in your presence is the one who is available for your compassion.

As the Vietnamese master Thich Nhat Hanh once observed:

> If you cannot make your own child happy, how do you expect to be able to make anyone else happy? If all our friends in the peace movement or of service communities of any kind do not love and help one another, whom can we love and help? Are we working for other humans, or are we just working for the name of an organization?

3. What Is the Most Important Thing to Do at All Times?

The compassionate actions of the hermit and the wise woman show that they both knew the answer to this question very well. Tolstoy concludes *Three Questions* by explaining why compassionate action toward the person in the moment is so highly esteemed: "because for that purpose alone was man sent into this life!" As we learned in the last chapter, doing *good* is the equivalent of doing *God*. We're not here to conquer others, wage war, build towering temples to our deities, become number one, win anything, or defeat anyone. No, we are here to be like God, or to be good—to serve, reach out, allow, not interfere, and be humble wherever we go.

Give your ego a rest and live compassionately by being a decent human being. The king learned this when he let go of his importance—by simply doing good, he saved his own life. And the woman in the mountains was able to teach an ego-driven man how to be happy by a simple demonstration of goodness.

Allow me to conclude this chapter by telling you another story, this one concerning my daughter Sommer and me. As I was driving her to the airport for her return to college after a long weekend home, she was admiring my new watch. Now this was the first new timepiece I'd had in at least a decade. I really enjoyed looking at its shiny steel-and-black face, and as I did, I'd think about how this was my favorite watch of all time. Yet I knew in my heart that Sommer would love to wear it, since men's watches seemed to be the current craze for young women.

As I dropped my daughter off at the curb and assisted her with her luggage, I was prompted to remove the watch and give it to her, even though it was my most prized possession (particularly since I have almost no possessions any longer that I even care about, let alone prize).

Sommer's response was, "No, Dad, you love this watch!"

I insisted, telling her that I'd feel greater joy by giving it to her and knowing she'd treasure it. I also said that I felt it would symbolize our staying together in time, even though we'd be thousands of miles apart. She boarded her plane glowing, and I left feeling that I had grown immeasurably as a person, since such a compassionate act would have been very difficult, if not impossible, for me several years ago.

Sommer called me in Maui a few months later to tell me that she was sending me a present for Father's Day, stressing that it was a very, *very* special gift. It turned out to be her all-time favorite painting that she'd created and had hung in her apartment for a long time. As she told me later: "I really learned something the day you gave me your beloved watch, and I wanted to give you something that's *my* single most precious item. I'm giving it to you, Dad, even though it's difficult to part with, because I want you to have a piece of me with you."

The painting hangs proudly on my wall as a symbol of the beauty and perfection of reaching out compassionately in response to a felt moment. This personal story epitomizes and personalizes the response to Tolstoy's three questions: (1) do it now, the only moment available; (2) do it with the person you're with in the moment; and (3) do good, because that is why you're here.

By being and living compassion, you invite and encourage others, just by your example, to choose to do the same.

Suggestions for Living from Compassion

— Upon awakening, let the words *Thank you* flow from your lips, for this will remind you to begin your day with gratitude and compassion. Make it a practice to begin each day by thinking first of someone else and then making a decision to actively do something, anything, that will bring a smile to his or her face. When you become conscious of wanting to do something kind for another human being, you move into a higher way of being. It takes your thoughts off yourself and *What's in it for me?* and puts them on *How may I serve?* which is precisely how the universal mind we call the Tao or God is always operating. When you're aligned with a compassionate outlook, your entire day will reflect this kind of awareness.

Here are some suggestions to get you started: e-mail a note of appreciation, say a kind word to one of your children with whom you've been having harsh words, apologize to an individual you've needed to make amends with, pick a few wildflowers and hand them to someone, give away some personal items such as books or jewelry, or send a smile toward someone that might brighten his or her moment. The point is that it doesn't have to cost money; what you're doing is aligning with compassion and thereby setting up your day to work in this way.

Whenever you find yourself employing one of your personally familiar excuses, you can stop yourself in midthought and immediately shift to the person you showed such humanity toward. Note how excuses disintegrate when your thoughts are on being kind toward others.

You needn't restrict your opening act of compassion to a person. All acts of kindness toward any of God's creatures, even if it's just picking up some trash that was carelessly discarded, impact our planet. The point is to set your mind on serving, and off of your ego's demands.

— In the quote that opens this chapter, Martin Luther King, Jr., suggests that our culture needs restructuring and that compassion is the way. I urge you to work toward electing people to public office—at all levels—who relate sensitivity and kindness in their messages to the public. Attitudes of compassion take into consideration men and women who are involved in concerns of immigration, torture, sexual orientation, religious persuasion, and socioeconomic status. There can be no exceptions here. Look for the compassionate heart, rather than the one that excludes, punishes, seeks revenge, or manipulates with government power. The more our institutions reflect this humane attitude, the fewer collective excuses we will call upon to explain why we haven't been able to create the heaven on earth that is our true calling.

— As I've stated in each of the seven principles in this part of the book, the active repetition of an inner mantra reinforces and creates exactly what you're saying to yourself. Therefore, repeat the following to yourself for at least five minutes: *I am a being of compassion. I extend love outward everywhere because this is my nature.* Affirm this to yourself continually, and post it in a prominent place in your home, your office, or even your car.

In the Sermon on the Mount, Jesus gives us the ultimate words of compassion. If our world today would put them into practice, we'd all be living in peace. But even if the rest of the world hasn't yet caught on, you can. I urge you to put these words to work in your life today; if you do, all excuses will most certainly vanish:

Ye have heard that it hath been said, Thou
shalt love thy neighbor, and hate thine enemy.

But I say unto you, Love your enemies, bless them
that curse you, do good to them that hate you, and pray
for them which despitefully use you, and persecute you
(Matthew 5:43–44).

This is compassion in action!

PART III

THE *EXCUSES BEGONE!*
PARADIGM SHIFT

*"If you correct your mind, the rest
of your life will fall into place."*

— Lao-tzu

CHAPTER 11

A NEW WAY OF LOOKING AT CHANGING OLD THINKING HABITS

"Never underestimate your power to change yourself.
Never overestimate your power to change others."

— H. Jackson Brown, Jr.

By now, you surely understand that you have the power to fundamentally change how your brain works, altering aspects of its chemistry to eradicate old mind viruses. You know that you can become a person who no longer relies upon excuses.

I've learned that what's true in nature is true for all humans in understanding ourselves. Just as the blossoms on a fruit tree fall away as the fruit grows, so does our need for a bouquet of rationalizations vanish as the Divine produces the authentic self. The more we allow ourselves to be guided by the principles that identify us as spiritual, the less we have any desire or inclination to use excuses. As Carl Jung put it: "Our most important problems cannot be solved; they must be outgrown."

Outgrow your need to ever use an excuse again. Even before you start putting the paradigm in this part of the book to work, do what you can to move beyond problems that are related to your old thinking habits. The principles I wrote about in Part II are designed to help you grow from a human being having a spiritual experience to the reverse: a spiritual being having a temporary human experience. This is what Jung meant by *outgrow*—something nature always does with its problems.

An acorn is just a tiny seed, a little nut that can't produce anything, yet as I'm fond of saying, "An infinity of forests lies dormant within the dreams of one acorn." An infinity of manifestations lies dormant within *you*, but you must get past the dormancy of your old thinking. So to aid you in doing this, here's a brief review of the seven *Excuses Begone!* principles I went through in Part II:

- Become *aware* of your potential for greatness and the power of your mind.

- *Align* yourself by thinking like God thinks.

- Live here and *now* in your mind as well as in your body.

- *Contemplate* what you are, rather that what you want to become.

- Be *willing* to allow health, happiness, and success to flow into your life.

- Be *passionate* about everyone and everything that enters your life.

- Want more for others than you do for yourself; that is, be *compassionate*.

These seven tools will help you outgrow your reliance on excuses and help you "correct your mind." When you're able to do this, as Lao-tzu reminded you a few pages ago, "the rest of your life will fall into place."

Yes, You Can Correct Your Mind!

In the first two chapters of this book, I described how a lot of time and effort has gone into convincing you to fit in and be like everybody else. That programming requires some effort on your part to overcome. As poet E. E. Cummings explains: "To be nobody-but-myself—in a world which is doing its best, night and day, to make you like everybody else—means to fight the hardest battle which any human being can fight, and never stop fighting."

You can accomplish being nobody-but-yourself without the actual fighting, although you may feel that you're battling something within yourself. As you let the Divine grow within you, however, you'll shift to a feeling of joy as the old discomfort retreats.

As a young person, you were inundated by a whole slew of "No you can't!" messages. These were subsequently internalized by you as *I can't* thoughts, which were buttressed by well-intentioned excuses. You internalized the notion that *I can't* because you were repeatedly told the following:

- "You'll never amount to anything."

- "You're worthless."

- "You're not smart enough."

- "You can never be good enough."

- "Money is hard to come by."

- "You don't deserve to succeed."

- "You'll never find someone to love you."

- "You'll probably get sick like your mother did; it's in your genes."

- "You'll never get ahead if you don't follow the rules."

- "You're just like your father, and he never amounted to anything."

These and thousands of variations on the same theme(s) seem to have erected permanent barriers within you. Excuses feel like they protect you from such awful sentiments, as well as the present disappointment with your life. Even though you've become an adult with no rational reason to hang on to such memes, they still produce a familiar reaction when it seems necessary to defend why your life isn't at the optimal level you'd prefer. And while you probably had no idea that these messages had infiltrated your brain, they nevertheless have a very strong pull on you.

Don't underestimate your power to change yourself, as the quote at the beginning of this chapter advises. You can absolutely overcome the internalized conviction of *I can't* so that it quickly becomes *I can* by affirming the following:

- *I can accomplish anything I choose.*

- *I am a worthy and valuable person.*

- *I am intellectually capable.*

- *I deserve the best because I am good.*

- *I attract abundance in all areas of my life.*

- *I deserve health, happiness, and success.*

- *I am loved by others, and I love myself.*

- *I am guided by my desire to serve others rather than following the rules.*

- *I am unique and independent of the good opinions of others.*

If you look closely at the preceding affirmations, you may note that they all represent a movement away from your old excuse-making mentality and toward thinking like God must think.

Seven Core Ideas for Eliminating Excuses

Before I explain the *Excuses Begone!* paradigm, I'd like to share with you a set of beliefs that I've adopted for myself. I encourage you to be receptive to these ideas, even if they initially seem inapplicable to your life at this time, because I feel strongly that they'll assist you in beginning the process of moving away from justification and defensiveness.

Here are the seven tips I've personally found to be very helpful in eradicating excuses from my life:

1. Remove Any and All Labels

Old habits of thinking stick around, often for an entire lifetime, largely because you create internal reasons to reinforce and maintain them. These reasons, which I'm calling "excuses," can become permanently lodged in your subconscious—they're labels you place on yourself that ultimately become your self-definition. In the words of Søren Kierkegaard, the famed Danish theologian: "Once you label me you negate me." As you enter the *Excuses Begone!* paradigm, make a promise to yourself that you won't be labeling *or* negating yourself anymore.

My daughter Serena grew up labeling herself as "not athletic" or even "frail," a self-definition that morphed into a comfortable excuse whenever physical activity came up. My daughter's labels negated the real Serena, who could become anything or anyone she chose. By consciously making a decision to remove those labels, and nothing more, Serena has gradually become a young woman who enjoys participating in athletic events and who loves the positive changes in her body as a result of daily exercise.

Rather than saddling yourself with self-limiting labels, affirm: *I am capable of accomplishing anything I place my attention upon.* Make it clear to yourself that you can never negate the real you; you're an infinite being, and with God all things are possible. The corollary of this would be: with labels, most things are negated!

2. Converse with Your Subconscious Mind

I refuse to accept the idea that we have an unconscious mind that defies us by being completely inaccessible. To me, this is a prescription for believing that for the major portion of our lives, we're controlled by unseen and unavailable forces residing within us. I recognize that we're often totally unaware of why we're behaving in certain ways, but this implies that we have no choice in the matter. *Awareness* is the simple key for alleviating this condition.

Have regular conversations with your subconscious—remind it that you don't want to go through life on automatic pilot. Discuss your unwillingness to be a victim of the whims of that "ghost in the machine" of your body, whose orders originate in the mind viruses and thinking habits that were programmed into it by people who are either long dead or no longer play a role in your adult life.

I usually tell my own habitual mind things like this: "I know that I have some really silly leftover habits that were instilled in me a long time ago, and I want you to know that I'm no longer interested in having my actions dictated by you. I'm bringing all of those old habits of thought to the surface, and I'm going to make a conscious effort to be more aware of all aspects of my life."

I had a conversation like this recently regarding my inclination to misplace my keys. I treated the ghost inside of me that always seemed to place my car keys in difficult-to-find locations as if it were a real person. While this may seem like an insignificant little habit, for me, changing it was huge. To this day I rarely misplace my keys.

Initiate a conversation with your subconscious mind in which you make it clear that you're not going to let part of your life be run by an invisible stranger who acts and reacts on the basis of memetic or genetic programming. Instead, decide that you're no longer going to allow (or excuse) behavior from an unconscious part of yourself.

3. Begin the Practice of Mindfulness

As you head into the seven chapters that identify a new paradigm for ridding yourself of excuses permanently, I encourage you to begin a practice of being more mindful. This is in fact what I did to end my lifetime habit of being forgetful, particularly when it came to where I placed my car keys.

At one time, I simply excused my can't-find-my-keys behavior with this label: "I'm forgetful." I can recall both my mother and my wife often exclaiming, "Oh, that's Wayne, our absentminded professor!" Memes buried within my subconscious became useful excuses for explaining my habit of being forgetful . . . but then I discovered how to be mindful. I began to practice being conscious of what I used to do unconsciously, and it worked!

Each time I came into the house, I made a decision to be aware of my keys in my hand—to feel the texture and shape of each one of them, to hold them with awareness, to listen to the jingle-jangle sound—and then place them in a special spot reserved just for them. And lo and behold, an old unconscious habit had been brought to the surface and into my conscious mind, causing that old excuse of being forgetful to be eradicated. (On the rare day when I can't find my keys now, it only serves to reinforce my commitment to stay mindful.)

By the same token, there was a time when my yoga practice could deteriorate into a boring routine and I'd become frustrated with myself; or while swimming in the ocean, running along the beach, or even sitting and writing, I could get lost in my old forgetfulness and lose sight of the glorious feeling that's available in all human activity. I found that practicing mindfulness in many ways throughout my day helped immensely.

In his book *The Miracle of Mindfulness,* Thich Nhat Hanh advises us on this practice:

> The Sutra of Mindfulness says, "When walking, the practitioner must be conscious that he is walking. When sitting, the practitioner must be conscious that he is sitting. When lying down, the practitioner must be conscious that he is lying down. . . ." The mindfulness of the positions of one's body is not enough, however. We must be conscious of each breath, each movement, every thought and feeling, everything which has any relation to ourselves.

These days when I swim, I experience my arms moving, my legs kicking, my shoulders stretching, the feel and taste of the salt water, my fingers cupped and moving the water, my breathing, my heart rate . . . all of it. Practicing mindfulness has taught me how to be in the moment and find my *self* as well as my keys!

That makes me think of a story Mobi Ho, a Vietnamese scholar who translated Hanh's book, tells:

> As I sat down to translate *The Miracle of Mindfulness,* I remembered the episodes during the past years that had nurtured my own practice of mindfulness. There was the time I was cooking furiously and could not find a spoon I'd set down amid a scattered pile of pans and ingredients. As I searched here and there, Thay [Hanh] entered the kitchen and smiled. He asked, "What is Mobi looking for?" Of course, I answered, "The spoon! I'm looking for a spoon!" Thay answered, again with a smile, "No, Mobi is looking for Mobi."

4. Commit to Overcoming Your Inertia

The excuses you frequently employ have taken up residence in your mind, which is dominated by your ego or false self; consequently, they won't simply pack up and leave without putting up a fight. Those excuses have become familiar companions with your ego, and they're always ready and willing to leap to your defense.

What I've found very useful in overcoming these ego-enriched justifications is to have a conversation with myself about who I intend to be and what I'm willing to do in order to bring this about. I call this my "commitment to overcoming inertia" conversation. I'm aware of my instinctive impulse to stay with the familiar, be inactive, and use the convenient excuses I delineated in Chapter 3. When it comes to fulfilling my commitment to complete a book at a certain time, for instance, I can always haul out, *I'm too busy . . . It's too big . . . It will take a long time . . . I really don't have the energy . . .* or what have you. Yet my inertia conversation helps me organize a few techniques to eliminate those excuses.

The first thing I do is draw up a contractual agreement with myself that I look at each day. After conversing with myself about overcoming inertia, I put a hand-drawn model of the book's jacket on my desk, so I'm writing from the perspective of acting as if what I want to complete is already here. I then continually remind myself that my word to my highest self (God) is sacred. This alone can push me in the direction of my writing space. Once I'm seated, all that procrastination—supported by excuses—disappears.

Before beginning the paradigm I explain in the next several chapters, I encourage you to make a commitment to give up inertia. Have a private conversation with your highest self and be willing to hold on to its vision for you, even if the old excuses come trotting back hoping for a sign of weakness on your part. The written agreement helps you recollect that you're in the process of redefining yourself. You are now practicing an *Excuses Begone!* philosophy for organizing and running your life.

5. Use the Power of Affirmations

You can make your entire living space an affirmation by having it reflect the energy you wish to utilize in fulfilling your personal destiny.

My own living space reflects what I wish to have in my life, and I've found this extraordinarily beneficial in underscoring my desire to cease using excuses of any kind. I affirm everything I am; all that I wish to become; and all that I treasure with written, photographic, artistic, and natural symbols of what I believe to be high energy sources.

I stay in alignment with this kind of energy by surrounding myself with what I wish to attract. For example, I want love in my life, so I place symbols of it around as affirmations that I'm aligned with what I want to receive. These include photographs that inspire thoughts of love, fresh flowers that are God's gifts of love in the form of natural beauty, books about love, and written statements such as these that I'm looking at as I write: "Love . . . binds everything together in perfect harmony" (Saint Paul); "He whom love touches not walks in darkness" (Plato); and "He who does not love does not know God, for God is love" (1 John 4:8).

Not only do you become what you think about all day long, you become what you avow to the universe as well. So before you start the *Excuses Begone!* paradigm in the following chapters, I urge you to make your home and working space living testimonials to your highest desires. Affirm that you're deserving of all the abundance that the universe has to offer. Affirm your love for yourself. Affirm that you're a Divine creation, and thus willing and open to that Divine Source working on your behalf.

Never underestimate the power affirmations hold in helping you eradicate the excuses you use to defend the shortcomings of your life.

6. Live in a Helpful, Supportive Universe

One of the most important decisions you'll ever make is choosing the kind of universe you exist in: is it helpful and supportive or hostile and unsupportive? Your answer to this question will make all the difference in terms of how you live your life and what kind of Divine assistance you attract.

Remember that you get what you think about, whether you want it or not. So if you're sure that this is an unfriendly universe, you'll look for examples to support this point of view. You'll anticipate people attempting to cheat, judge, take advantage of, and otherwise harm you. You'll blame the antagonistic, inhospitable cosmos for not cooperating with you in the fulfillment of your desires. You'll point the finger at belligerent folks and bad luck for the kind of world we all live in. Since this worldview trickles down into every thought you have, you become a person persistently looking for occasions to be offended, and therefore in possession of a whole slew of excuses.

I implore you to see the universe as a warm and supportive one before you begin to apply the *Excuses Begone!* paradigm, because you'll look for evidence to support this view. When you believe that the universe is friendly, you see friendly people. You look for circumstances to work in your favor. You expect good fortune flowing into your life. In other words, you aren't looking for excuses!

My favorite affirmation when I feel stuck or out of sorts is: *Whatever I need is already here, and it is all for my highest good.* Jot this down and post it conspicuously throughout your home, on the dashboard of your car, at your office, on your microwave oven, and even in front of your toilet! Remind yourself: *I live in a friendly universe that will support any thing or desire that is aligned with the universal Source of all.* Such a stance will be a giant step toward living an *Excuses Begone!* life.

Affirming that what you want is already here and all you have to do is connect to it causes you to remember that what you attract is for your highest good, so you can then let go of the timing issue altogether. Just know that it is here and will arrive on God's schedule—as does everything that makes the journey from nonbeing to being.

I've found that by shifting my belief about the nature of the universe, I attract whatever I desire into my life. I desire love. I desire peace. I desire health. I desire happiness. I desire prosperity. Why would I want to hold the view that our universe is unsupportive, evil, and unfriendly? How could I expect the Divine realm to hear me if I'm asking it to be something other than what it is? Thus, I see my desires in perfect rapport with how the universe works.

When I pray, I do so in the spirit of Saint Francis. Rather than ask God to grant him peace, this inspiring man beseeched God to "make me an instrument of Thy peace." In other words, "Let me be like the Source from which I originated, and then I will rest in the knowing that it must be here, on its way, and for my highest good." As you can see, there's no room for excuses when you apply this model to your everyday life.

As I've written and said many times, "When you change the way you look at things, the things you look at change." And this applies to the entire universe.

7. Don't Complain—Don't Explain!

Complaining and explaining are the two huge allies of excuse making. Generally speaking, when you resort to complaining you employ an excuse of one kind or another, placing the responsibility for what's upsetting you on something or someone external to yourself. Complaining about the way somebody has performed (or failed to perform) is another way of making an excuse for why you're dissatisfied or unhappy. "It's their fault that my blood pressure is up—look at how miserably they've performed" or, "How can I enjoy myself at dinner when everyone here at this restaurant is behaving so incompetently?" are prime examples. Finding fault with circumstances, the weather, the economy, other people, or anything else outside yourself is a way to hang on to excuses.

In addition to putting an end to complaints, I recommend that you never attempt to explain. As I've pursued a no-excuses mentality, I've made it my policy to keep the things that I wish to accomplish a private matter. By doing so, I'm never forced into a stance of having to explain myself. I'm well aware that many of my personal life missions sound strange and outrageous to others. Consequently, I've learned to avoid sharing my intentions with anyone, outside of a select few whom I know and trust at a spiritual level. (Anything I might say to these individuals wouldn't require me to explain myself in any way.)

The problem with having to explain yourself is that in doing so, you inevitably invoke the ego to do your bidding. You have a tendency to make yourself right, sensible, and understood; while at the same time dealing with the doubts and antagonisms of those who don't share your views or your optimism. When you keep things to yourself, you stay connected to your spiritual side, or the place within you that has no need to be right or to make anyone else wrong.

Since all of creation comes from the world of nonbeing, if you want to give life to your dreams and desires—if you wish to manifest your own destiny—then you must rely on the great Source of all creation, Spirit. The moment you inject ego into the picture, you invite excuses; and the moment you invoke those familiar excuses, you stop the creative and the creation process from manifesting.

As Lao-tzu put it:

The Tao gives rise to all forms, yet it has no form of its own . . .
Stop striving after admiration.
Place your esteem on the Tao.
Live in accord with it,
share with others the teachings that lead to it,
and you will be immersed in the blessings that flow from it.[2]

In more modern language, stop complaining and explaining—your excuses will soon cease.

These, then, are my seven favorite ideas for you to contemplate as you prepare to study the *Excuses Begone!* paradigm.

How to Use the Paradigm

I created the *Excuses Begone!* paradigm because of my strong belief in the spirit of the quote at the beginning of this chapter: "Never underestimate your power to change yourself. Never overestimate your power to change others." The key word in this quotation is *power*. I know there's a power within you that's capable of making dramatic changes in relatively short periods of time.

The problem I've discovered is that most people feel disempowered when it comes to overcoming a lifetime of self-defeating thinking. It's actually quite easy to change the way we think and act, regardless of how long we've done it or how much reinforcement we've received that's solidified a way of being. I've put myself to this test on many occasions, and I've always found that making these changes is much simpler than others would have me think. I believe that in the same way our body knows how to maintain an optimal state of health without any outside interference, so too is our mind programmed by Source energy to know how and what to think in order to optimize our emotional and spiritual development.

I have stopped underestimating the power we contain within us to make apparently radical shifts and have applied the *Excuses Begone!* paradigm to overcome addictions of all stripes in my life. I've also used it to help me attract the right people, the right circumstances, the right jobs, the funding I needed, the healing I desired, and so on. I've seen many individuals leave old thinking and behavior behind with very little time or hard effort devoted to the outcome. The impact of early imprinting and conditioning is felt throughout life until a change is initiated, but I've never bought into the idea that our early-childhood programming is insurmountable. Nor do I accept that we have an unconscious mind that cannot be accessed. And you know that I even reject the idea that our genes and DNA are excuses for all manner of thinking and behaving. Rather, I've chosen to believe in the innate power within each of us to change.

Each chapter that follows in this last part of this book is presented as a question to ask yourself. Take some time before you answer, and read through the chapters with a mind that's open to everything and attached to nothing. Consider the examples I present, examine both sides, and stay neutral in your assessment of how they apply to you today. In other words, simply let it all come in—particularly the parts that you immediately think don't apply to you!

There are no exercises to do, lists to make, rules to follow, or complicated instructions to memorize. All you need to do as you read the following pages is keep in mind the words of Lao-tzu: "If you correct your mind, the rest of your life will fall into place." This paradigm for changing habituated thinking is all about helping you to correct your mind. Enjoy, as everything else just falls into place.

CHAPTER 12

THE FIRST QUESTION:
IS IT TRUE?

"I shall try to correct errors when shown to be errors, and I shall adopt new views so fast as they shall appear to be true views."

— Abraham Lincoln

I've heard estimates, from those who engage in such accounting practices, that the average adult has approximately 60,000 separate thoughts in a 24-hour period. Even more startling is that we think the *same* 60,000 thoughts today that we had yesterday and will have tomorrow. Thus, many of us go through our daily lives in a habituated pattern, endlessly repeating the same thoughts over and over again!

Now let me add a bit of fuel to this firestorm. I suggest that the vast majority of those continually reiterated notions, particularly those that fall into the excuse category, are very likely untrue. It then follows that we use our incomparably brilliant minds to obliviously process false thoughts on a daily basis. *Is it true?* has to be the first challenge to this repetitious, habitual, and unconscious activity of making excuses.

This first question in the *Excuses Begone!* paradigm will lead you to an awareness of the personal nature of your justifications. When you discover how your mind selects untrue thoughts to guide you, you'll also reveal a major impetus to ending that habit that has held you back from so much in life.

Finding the Truth in Four Popular Excuses

If you were to discover that a thought you use to define who you are to yourself and others is false, would you want to continue using it? Obviously I've posed this as a rhetorical question, since readers of a book titled *Excuses Begone!* probably don't want to hang on to anything that is preventing them from improving their quality of life. It's far more beneficial and desirable to be guided by the simple teaching that the truth shall set you free. So be open to the truth as you read this chapter—your honest answers will assist you enormously in unearthing your thought patterns.

The question *Is it true?* demands that you determine whether or not you can be absolutely certain that those mental crutches you've been relying on are indeed accurate. If they're not, then you must decide right away to invalidate them—using these excuses to hold you back from what you're drawn to do or be is akin to running your life on the basis of a lie.

In the earliest days of our democracy, Thomas Paine wrote: "But such is the irresistible nature of truth that all it asks, and all it wants, is the liberty of appearing." This suggests that the truth only wants to show up; it doesn't wish to overwhelm or rule us. So let's allow "the irresistible nature of truth" to make its appearance right now.

Under close scrutiny, the old familiar explanations almost always turn out to be false, so it's important to test their truth. Here, I'll use 4 of the 18 excuse categories I detailed in Chapter 3 to illustrate working with the first question in our new paradigm:

1. It Will Be Difficult

This is certainly one of the most common excuses. Such a meme keeps you from fulfilling your highest vision, but is it even correct? Are you 100 percent certain that what you wish to accomplish is going to be a challenge? Is it plausible that what you desire isn't actually difficult but might in fact require very little effort? While you may feel that isn't likely, you have to admit that the *possibility* of its being easy rather than hard is real.

Keep in mind that all of the seemingly impossible happenings that occur under the guise of what Carl Jung called "synchronicity" do so with a kind of ease and an inexplicably bizarre twist of fate, in which little or no effort is expended. This happens to us all quite frequently, particularly when we're more aligned with Spirit than the material world. There seems to be a collaboration with destiny, and a magical connection takes place making what was perceived to be hard rather easy.

If the thought *It's going to be difficult* might not be true, then something could very well occur to make it not be difficult, which means that the habituated meme is false. So now you have a choice with this excuse: (a) you can believe a thought *(It's going to be difficult)* that is very likely false and most assuredly preventing you from accomplishing what you want; or (b) you can believe an opposite thought *(It will be easy)* that could also be false yet still assists you in fulfilling your desire. When there's a choice, the notion that something is possible or easy is hands down more inviting than the one that insists it's impossible or difficult. So which thought do you wish to hold?

I recall the advice that I received concerning getting my first textbook published a year or so after completing my doctoral studies. This is what I kept hearing: "It's sure going to be hard," "Getting published is impossible," "You're unknown—who would want to publish what you, a 30-year-old novice, has to say?" and the like. Yet I never bought into that logic; consequently, I didn't adopt the *It's going to be difficult* excuse meme. I sent out 100 copies of my manuscript, and within a week I had 99 rejection letters

. . . but I also had an offer from a small publisher in New Jersey. Essentially, what others thought of as a challenge didn't strike me as such. I knew instinctively that someone somewhere would be interested in what I had to say, and it all came about with relative ease.

I also recall quite clearly my experience getting national publicity for *Your Erroneous Zones,* my first book written for the general public, in 1976. The experts all proclaimed that it was next to impossible to get booked on *The Tonight Show, The Phil Donahue Show,* the *Today* show, and so on; this ready-made excuse would have been as good a reason as any to give up.

As it turned out, Howard Papush, a talent coordinator on *The Tonight Show,* read *Your Erroneous Zones* on a flight from New York to Los Angeles. He called me to come out for a preinterview, and I was booked on the program a week later. Over the next three years, I made 37 appearances on *The Tonight Show,* and I was a guest on virtually every other national talk show as well. It turns out that this first excuse didn't apply at all—it was actually quite easy to get national media coverage. I only had to answer the phone!

So once again, if the belief that *It will be difficult* isn't 100 percent true, why would you choose to support that notion? Not once in 1976 did I say that getting on a national TV show would be hard. I trusted that the universe would provide experiences that matched my desires, and that it would all work out for my highest good. The most important point is that by staying aligned with this thinking, I had no need to fall back on a tired old (and untrue) excuse.

2. There Will Be Family Drama

This is one of those rationales people employ all the time to explain why they feel stuck or otherwise precluded from living the life they desire. On and on go the reasons for staying put and doing the bidding of family members: "My parents would have a fit," "Everyone would be so upset with me," "No one in my entire family has ever done such a thing," "I'd be labeled a troublemaker or a rebel," "No one has ever stood up to my father before—it would be a nightmare," and so forth.

If you tend to use this excuse, ask yourself: *Can I be 100 percent certain that there will be family drama if I take the action I'm contemplating? Does the possibility exist that I could do the thing I desire and not generate any outbursts?* If the potential exists that there won't be any problems, then this excuse has to go into the "not true" category.

The opposite thought of *There will be family drama* is *There will be no family drama if I carry out my plans as I would like them to unfold.* You may think that without this excuse, you'd automatically be placed on the risky path of doing something that you've been avoiding. But think again! You have a choice to believe that there will either be a family disruption or there won't. Since either one has the potential to be true, why not opt for the thought that could bring about your desired result?

By staying aligned with the idea of loved ones who will both understand and support you in your desire, you may very well see that happen. Or your relatives could indeed react in the disconcerting way that your excuse predicted. But which thought do you think is more likely to produce the kind of results you'd like to have? The point is that you cannot be absolutely certain of what this excuse predicts, so I urge you not to select an explanation for your habituated behavior that's most assuredly untrue.

I can tell you with some degree of certainty that by not expecting to be impacted in a negative or fearful way, you have a much better chance of eliciting the reaction you want. You have a higher chance of your family members being supportive when you support your own desires and intentions. And do be willing to endure any disapproval you might face by asserting your strong beliefs about your purpose in life—that disapproval will most assuredly morph into respect, gratitude, and even awe.

In my own life, I know that if I fail to show up for a cousin's wedding, an uncle's funeral, a grandchild's birthday party, or any other family occasion, there will be no drama for me to withstand.

I've shown my relatives that I'm uninterested in dealing with censure or nagging, so I never have to use this second excuse.

You can bid adieu to this excuse yourself by simply asking: *Is it 100 percent true that my loved ones will disapprove if I _____?* Since you can't guarantee family drama all of the time, revise your thoughts to reflect that there won't be any, period. Now, you can't be certain that *some* turbulent or emotional episodes won't occur, but at least you've set your mind on what you desire, and you're aligned with the idea of a peaceful family response. Cement your new reality by affirming: *What I desire is already present and on its way.*

When you eliminate the belief that *There will be family drama* from your life entirely, you'll once again be reminded of what happens when you stay aligned with an expectation of the higher energy of peace, tranquility, and love. You'll be so much more likely to see this peaceful attitude emerge than if you're angry, frustrated, and hurt because "no one ever understands" you in your family.

3. I Can't Afford It

I've always held a different concept about my ability to create the necessary financing for anything I've wanted or needed. As you're probably aware, my background is foster homes, scarcities, economic depression, and having to work for everything I've ever had from the age of nine with my first paper route; yet I've never allowed myself to use this third excuse.

Let's examine this very common meme to see if it's true. Can you be 100 percent certain that you're unable to afford whatever it is that you would like to accomplish or purchase? If there's any doubt in your mind, no matter how unlikely prosperity may seem to you now, then you must reject this excuse. The opposite of *I can't afford it* is *I can afford it, even if I don't know at the moment how I can make it all come true financially.*

Once again, the importance of this question regarding your ability to raise money becomes evident. If the thought *I can afford it* is true or false, and the same can be said of *I can't afford it,* then why opt for the idea that's almost guaranteed to keep you from reaching your goal?

Perhaps you're convinced that you're in a position of being insolvent and unable to attract the financing for your dreams. One of the basic tenets of an *Excuses Begone!* mentality is that you get what you think about, whether you want it or not. Therefore, thinking about a dearth of cash aligns you with the concept of shortage and lack. The more you focus on what you don't have and can't get, the more you provide the universe with opportunities to offer up experiences that reflect those beliefs. By claiming that you can't afford something, you confirm this expectation (which, by the way, is just as likely to be untrue as it is to be true). The belief itself becomes the source of what you attract—it serves as an obstacle to a universe of unlimited abundance.

I'm sorry to tell you that there's no solution for scarcity-focused thought processes. Rather, you have to *outgrow* this kind of immature thinking by reminding yourself that it makes much more sense to assert that you're prosperous instead of focusing on *I can't afford it.* Attract the universal guidance that will help rather than the kind that hinders. Right here, right now, state: "I can never be absolutely certain that the financing I need or desire is not on its way. Thus, the belief *I can't afford it* is false, and I refuse to let myself use this excuse."

This is not about helping you manifest more money, although that's certainly a possibility. It's about helping you eliminate the excuse of *I can't afford it* from your life, because using it keeps you aligned with lack, shortages, and pain. Loving what you have and being in a continuous state of contentment is the key to having what you want. Also, be willing to contemplate that whatever assistance you need is on its way, even when you can't predict where it's coming from. This helps you live in alignment with the laws of the universe. Since this is a universe of unlimited abundance, why have thoughts contrary to that truth?

I've always said that what I need financially is not only on its way, but will arrive on time and is always for my highest good.

In fact, it already exists—all I have to do is connect myself to it. Call me crazy if you will, but this kind of thinking has served me unfailingly. The falsity of *I can't afford it* is even more pronounced now in my 60s as I stay unattached to what comes my way and offer it to others in as generous a fashion as I can. This doesn't mean that I simply open the windows and money flies in; rather, it allows me to act on thoughts that have no room for scarcity. I act on what I believe, and I refuse to believe that money is a reason not to do anything.

Throughout my life, I've been surprised on many occasions when financing for a project of mine just seemed to manifest out of nowhere. When I was a young sailor who desperately wanted to attend college after my enlistment, for instance, the funding wasn't immediately available. Nevertheless, I acted upon my strong intention to attend a major university by putting 90 percent of my savings into a special bank account on Guam. Upon my honorable discharge from a four-year tour of duty, I had enough money in the bank to pay for my four years of college.

The point is that making the choice to take advantage of thinking *I can afford it* allows the following two things to happen: (1) universal cooperation is activated by aligning with a universe that has no limits or shortages; and (2) you begin to act on what you're thinking about.

4. No One Will Help Me

This excuse belongs in the blame category. Is it always someone else's fault that you're unable to manifest the happiness, success, and health you'd like? Do other people keep letting you down? Does it seem as if it's next to impossible to get things done because you can't find anybody to lend you a hand? I'm not suggesting that you're unable to accomplish your dreams without the assistance of others; rather, I'd like you to consider the validity of the premise that there's no one there to help you.

Put this fourth excuse to the truth test. Ask yourself if you can be 100 percent certain that there won't be anyone out there to help you or that you're in this all alone. If any possibility at all exists that there *are* people to help you, then you must reject this belief as a falsehood that you've chosen to use as a guidepost for your life. The fact is that there's a limitless number of potential helpers out there, but they may be kept away from you because you keep trying to validate an incorrect belief. Revise this excuse by affirming: *Whatever help I require will show up when I need it, and I trust that it is already here and on its way to help me fulfill my highest good.* This kind of thinking is just as likely to be true or false as your original excuse is, so why not go with it? Such a favorable notion aligns you with how the universe truly works.

There are billions of human beings on this planet, so why conclude that there's no one to help you accomplish what you feel called upon to create? The answer lies in the blame game, which is a meme planted in your mind by others who have been plagued by mind viruses, too. It's just as likely that aid will be there when you need it as it is that it won't be there. So what's the point of using precious mental energy on an excuse that's much more likely to produce an undesirable outcome? You have the option of using that same energy to produce a *desirable* outcome.

Shift your focus off of yourself and your ego desires and on to *How may I serve?* When you want for others what you'd like to have for yourself, you'll find that there's never a shortage of helpful, friendly, kind, understanding folks who can't seem to do enough for you. For every act of evil, anger, hatred, or indifference in the world, there are a million acts of kindness, assistance, and love. Choose to place your attention on all that is good and be done with this falsehood: *No one will help me.* If you're looking for "no one" to support you, I can guarantee you that the universe will present you with experiences mirroring your low expectations. On the other hand, if you believe that you're aligned with supportive energy, that's what will show up.

Let go of this excuse by recognizing and reminding yourself that the belief that no one will be there for you does not hold up to the test of truth: there's no one to blame, and there are thousands of people out there who would love to offer you the aid and guidance you desire. Choose instead to know that you live in a universe that supports you at all times.

Thomas Merton once wrote: "We cannot possess the truth fully until it has entered into the very substance of our life by good habits . . ." And that is precisely what the first question of the *Excuses Begone!* paradigm is designed to do. That is, it aims to help you eliminate counterproductive habits of thinking that are untrue but have become the substance of your life. The truth really will set you free. You no longer need excuse making, because the explanations you've been using for why your life isn't working simply don't hold up to the truth test.

If you go through the 18 excuses in Chapter 3 (you just reviewed 4 of them) and examine each of them closely, you'll find that you can't give an unqualified yes to the question that's the topic of this chapter: *Is it true?*

If you have a choice to use an excuse that may or may not be false and will keep you stuck in place, or to use a different explanation that still may or may not be false but leads you out of self-defeating thinking habits, which choice should you make? To me, the answer is obvious. Your goal is to develop habits that serve you and enhance your opportunity to maximize your success, happiness, and health—and that means eschewing those old excuses, which are just plain lies.

Suggestions for Applying the First Paradigm Question

— Whenever you're tempted to use an excuse to explain some deficiency in your life (or even after you've noticed that you just relied on a long-standing alibi), silently put the excuse to the truth test. Simply and honestly answer these two questions: (1) *Is it true?* and (2) *Can I be 100 percent certain that it's true?* As you do, you'll discover that no excuse pattern holds up to this scrutiny.

Even if you don't fully understand how you're going to accomplish this, tell yourself that you don't wish to continue vindicating yourself with false notions. This simple truth test will lead to further exploration of what else you can do to eliminate excuses.

— Create an explanation that reverses the excuse you're using. It should be just as capable of being either true or untrue as your mental crutch, but the difference is that this explanation leads you away from self-defeat.

Here's an example of what I mean:

Excuse: *I'm too old to pursue my college degree.*

Question: *Is it true?*

Answer: *It may be true, but it also may not be true.*
I can't be 100 percent certain that such a
statement is rock-solid, guaranteed truth.

In order to demolish this excuse that's been keeping you from pursuing a college degree, create the opposite thought of *I am the perfect age to pursue my college degree.* By holding on to this new belief, which indeed may or may not be 100 percent true, you open a world of possibilities. The bonus is that you align yourself with the field of all possibilities and invite reinforcements to help you.

Since neither your old excuse nor your new belief can be 100 percent guaranteed, and you're free to hold either of these two visions for yourself, why not select the one that will work *for* the highest aspirations you hold, rather than against them? The creative Source that birthed you from nonbeing to being supports you in this endeavor. As it says in the Bible: "Trust in the Lord with all your heart, and lean not on your own understanding; in all your ways acknowledge Him, and He shall direct your paths" (Proverbs 3:5–6).

Your insight has led you to all of the excuses you've relied on for a good part of your life. The "Him" in Proverbs is God (or the eternal Tao), which is the ultimate truth. Be receptive to revising your excuse formula; it may indeed be God calling you to His truth.

Henry Ward Beecher offers heady advice on distinguishing what's true from what's false: "Pushing any truth out very far, you are met by a counter truth." I recommend giving just as much attention to the "counter truth" as you have to the excuses you've been treating as truth.

CHAPTER 13

THE SECOND QUESTION: *WHERE DID THE EXCUSES COME FROM?*

"Nor deem the irrevocable Past
As wholly wasted, wholly vain,
If, rising on its wrecks, at last
To something nobler we attain."

— Henry Wadsworth Longfellow

When you go to your doctor with a medical problem, you're prepared to answer questions designed to help him or her determine what's going on and what treatment plan to initiate. One important function of this inquiry is to assist your physician in understanding what brought about the illness, infection, or trauma. I'm going to use this medical model as a metaphor to explore the question *Where did the excuses come from?* in relation to making them vanish from your life.

Getting to the Bottom of Your Excuses

When it comes to those mental crutches you've relied upon for so many years, it will help you to become your own doctor and to learn the origin and duration of your "condition" before you implement treatment. Just like physical problems, habituated thinking patterns that keep you from attaining the life of your dreams can be remedied by knowing how and why they occurred, and a program of prevention can then be instituted.

Using the same model of an "intake interview" that your medical doctor would conduct, here are five questions that will help you understand where your excuses come from:

1. What Are Your Symptoms?

Imagine the excuses you've employed as symptoms that have been keeping you from maximizing your potential for happiness, success, and health—even if they may not be as obvious as a fever, a runny nose, a sore throat, or any other physical symptom that would cause you to seek out medical attention.

Describe what you're feeling when you know you've got the excuse bug, and be as specific as you can. Common symptoms include: frequent episodes of blame and faultfinding, when just about anyone or anything that you think of is held responsible for your unhappiness; shame that sneakily attacks you; anger at yourself and others, which erupts at the tiniest irritation; envy that breaks out when you compare yourself to others; and laziness, inactivity, and complaining. As the excuse bug takes hold, you notice that you spend a lot of time looking for occasions to be offended—anyone else's success, happiness, and good health just serve to intensify your symptoms. Self-doubt, resentment, anxiety, worry, hopelessness, sadness, unworthiness, and more may also occur.

2. When Did Your Symptoms First Appear?

Your symptoms could very well stem from childhood memories that still persist in adult versions. For example, the rationalization *I'm too old* may have appeared as *I'm too young* when you were a teenager; and the adult excuse *I'm too busy* might have originated as *I can't play with my friends because I have to do my chores, study, and get to bed* when you were in school. Perhaps you also admired family members who modeled seemingly successful excuse-making behavior.

These lifelong thinking habits have become so incorporated into your being that only now are you beginning to see them as symptomatic of a disease process. While there's no remedy for the conditions you were exposed to that contributed to the presence of your "excuses disease" today, you can now see how you were infected at an early age. And the best medicine for this situation may just be found in humor like actress Tallulah Bankhead's, particularly in the observation she was said to have made that "the only thing I regret about my past is the length of it. If I had to live my life again I'd make the same mistakes, only sooner."

3. Whom Were You With?

Simply knowing whom you were with when you came down with your excuses disease unfortunately won't change it. You'll gain a modicum of insight, but the conclusion remains the same: your past is always going to be the way it was, and there's no way to alter it.

Those people you were with when you caught so many self-defeating thinking habits should be pretty obvious to you by now. They include members of your immediate and extended family, especially your parents and grandparents; teachers, classmates, and friends; members of religious organizations; and even folks who appeared on the televison programs you watched, in the magazines and newspapers you read, and in the music you listened to.

I could go on and on listing all of the ways you were exposed to mind viruses. The only purpose those viruses had was to replicate, infiltrate, and spread wherever possible—and your inquisitive, open, and willing mind surely was an inviting place for them to take up residence.

So when you ask whom you were with when you caught the excuses disease, you can realistically answer that it was most everyone and everything you came into regular contact with from the earliest moments of your life.

4. Did the People You Were Around Have Similar Symptoms? Were They Contagious?

If you were being medically treated for a disease, it would be important to curtail its spread—not only would you need to be treated accordingly, but whomever you caught it from would need to be, too. In addition, you'd be told how to minimize endangering others, and you might even be isolated to stop the epidemic from growing.

The people with whom you had close contact throughout your life carried the illness of excuse making. Obviously, medication or isolation aren't called for here, but you *do* need to make the decision to rehabilitate yourself if you are to overcome lifelong habituated thinking habits.

While you were growing up and being exposed to the excuses disease, you were unaware of what was happening. The means for transferring the mind viruses you caught was through the magic of memetics, which I discussed in the opening chapters of this book. Remember that *mimic* is the root word of *memetics,* and you certainly did mimic the infected people around you. You were a ready, willing, and gullible little package for the memes to take root, replicate, and spread in. If your environment hadn't been so fertile, you wouldn't be dealing with the effects of those excuses today.

This isn't a reason to blame anyone—there were lots of opportunities, particularly as you grew into your teen years and beyond, when you had a choice in allowing the excuses to take hold or not. Rather, this is all about seeing that in your earliest years, you were a magnet for the energy that was directed at you. And as you got older, you didn't exactly stop pulling excuses toward you and start attracting and nourishing the ways that would have allowed you to outgrow them.

5. Were You Exposed?

The short answer here is *yes*. Of course you were exposed, because you had daily contact with carriers of mind viruses. However, the *Excuses Begone!* paradigm is designed to strengthen your natural immune system so that you can deal with any similar disease processes that may come your way, now and in the future.

Accepting Total Responsibility

In spite of your history, the one and only place that your excuses originated is in you. Regardless of the age you were when these ideas were implanted; how contagious your early family conditioning was; how frequently you were exposed; and how potent the diseases were in your home, school, church, and culture, the responsibility is yours. To live a totally excuse-free life, you must be willing to state: "I adopted these behaviors—I chose all of it. I may have been a child, and I may not have had the skills or natural abilities to resist early influences, but it was still my choice. I take full responsibility for any and all excuse making that I've engaged in."

The reason I took you through the five questions in the last section wasn't so you could find new explanations for your habit, but rather so you could see just how prevalent mind viruses were during the formative years of your life. Now, at each stage of exposure to these mind viruses, there was always you. You may have been vulnerable, gullible, fearful, wanting to fit in, or just going along with the program, but there was still *you*. You're not a chair that's been redesigned and reupholstered or a robot that was created in a laboratory and oiled to perfection by its owners . . . no, you're a live human being with a mind of your own. After all, other members of your family—perhaps even some of your siblings—weren't fooled like you were, and you probably saw some of your friends resist the efforts of others to enculturate them in this manner.

I encourage you to accept complete responsibility for all of your excuse-making tendencies. You are capable of making choices to cease self-sabotaging thinking habits now, and you were just as capable when you were a child. Yet please don't take responsibility with any sense of shame or self-reproach. Know that throughout your life, you always did what you knew how to do; you're also not currently being punished or attracting these inclinations because of some past-life karmic debt. I elaborated the excuse-building symptoms and the contagious effect of those early memes so that you can understand them, give them a fond embrace, and bid them all farewell! Think about what Saint Paul said in his Letter to the Corinthians: "When I was a child . . . I thought like a child" (1 Cor. 13:11). Look back at those early childlike mimicking behaviors and remind yourself: *I no longer need to hang on to anything I adopted as a young person, regardless of how powerful the influences may have been.*

When you ask *Where did these excuses come from?* the answer is that they came from you, an individual who was once willing to listen to that kind of thinking. But avow that you now intend to say good-bye and good riddance to excuses that keep you from experiencing the highest, most glorious levels of happiness, success, and health.

The key concept to grasp here is that once you start understanding, you can stop rationalizing and justifying. Your past isn't another reason to explain your deficiencies—don't tell yourself that old influences are your excuse for making excuses! Take responsibility for your life, and discontinue the use of blame and faultfinding.

Let's take a look at 4 of the 18 excuses from Chapter 3 to illustrate how your excuse-making habit has been shaped:

1. I Don't Deserve It

How is it possible for a Divine creation to be unworthy? You are and always have been a piece of God. And you know by now that all beings come from nonbeing; the Bible itself reminds you that it's Spirit that gives life. So where on earth did you learn to use this excuse?

As a developing child, you were weaned on ideas that your worthiness is based on ego-dominated formulations making you what you do, what you have, and what others think of you. Your worth became intertwined with these ego constructs: *If I do well, I'm worthy; if I don't, I'm unworthy. If I accumulate more valuable stuff and make more money, I'm worthy; if I don't, I'm unworthy. If I gain the approval of others, I'm worthy; if I'm unpopular, I'm unworthy.*

Like most of us, you were immersed in a culture that taught and reinforced these ideas, which are the work of the false self. Consequently, as an adult, when you see others who are more successful than you are, have more toys than you do, and enjoy reputations far greater than yours, your first impulse is to make a disconnect between your status in life and your worthiness as a human being. Years of solid training in ego development have caused you to retreat into an *I don't deserve it/I'm not worthy* mindset. Since these excuses come from the false self, they'll stay with you until you leave the planet, unless you're willing to tell yourself: "Okay, I understand where this kind of egotistic reasoning originated—and I can see that I still use it—but I'm practicing the *Excuses Begone!* way of life from now on."

For every one of these excuse categories, I urge you to decide to start thinking something along the lines of this: *Everyone in my life did what they knew how to do, and I chose to buy into it at that time. But today I'm going to stop this insidious kind of absurd thinking and remind myself that I'm a Divine being, an individualized expression of God. Therefore, I will no longer entertain thoughts of my being unworthy—I've lived with them long enough, and they've never served my highest good.*

2. It's Not My Nature

Have you been allowed to develop as if your Creator were in charge of the process? Of course your physical shell was permitted to take the course nature dictated: you developed the height; body type and shape; hair, eye, and skin color; and facial features that nature called for. But what about your personality, your emotional and intellectual development, your aspirations, your self-concept, or your spiritual awareness—were those aspects of you encouraged to unfold naturally?

The excuse *It's not my nature* came directly from the list of what you were taught you couldn't do or be that I elaborated earlier in this book. You were formulated and then crafted into the finished product that your family and culture desired. When you're told "You can't do this; you can only do that" enough times, and you're willing to become the product the people around you want you to be, then you believe that your nature is what you've been told. You act on the pronouncements about yourself that you've absorbed. So if you hear that you're lazy, undeserving, or uncoordinated often enough, it ultimately leads you to adopt this as your self-portrait. If you're told over and over again that you're just like your father and he never amounted to anything, then you'll ultimately view your nature the way that others viewed your dad.

Go back to the question I asked you earlier in this book: *Who would you be if you didn't have anyone to tell you who you are?* Take total responsibility for whatever you believe constitutes your nature, reminding yourself to think in a fresh way about where this excuse originated. Try something like: *I chose to allow the opinions of others to be more important than my fledgling opinions of who I was and what I intended to become. Yes, I was small and vulnerable, but it was still my choice.* This kicks the old excuse down the stairs and helps you love the person you were then, causing you to tenderly undo what you (not someone else) have done. While you can never change the actions of others, taking responsibility for your own life will help you make the shift to an *Excuses Begone!* existence.

182

3. I'm Not Smart Enough

Where do you think you learned that you were somewhat shortchanged in the brains department? Well, you were enrolled in an educational system that assigned numbers to your intellectual capacity. A test gave you an IQ number to carry around for life. You learned to listen to a teacher whose lesson plan wasn't designed for the variety of learning modes in the classroom, so all of the students were being exposed to the same instruction. At the end of the week, an exam gave you a grade that measured you against the performances of all of your classmates; you all had your place on a bell-shaped curve depending on your aptitudes that day, in that week, and on that particular subject area. You developed a self-image based on what teachers, test scores, and academic performance indicated—you learned that you were average at spelling, above average in art, but mentally challenged in mathematics. Soon you had the makings of a great excuse *(I'm not smart enough)* that you hauled out whenever it was convenient.

What you failed to learn is that intelligence tests only measure how well you take intelligence tests! It turns out that academic performance has nothing to do with your potential for intellectual mastery. Nonetheless, your young mind hung on to those school experiences and added them to the messages you'd already absorbed about how you're not as smart as your siblings, you've never been good at figuring out numerical problems, or you're not as talented as the kids next door. This cascade of criticism directed at your intellectual capacities can easily lead you to defend yourself from these jabs with excuses.

The fact is that since you're a creation who originated in the world of Spirit, you have exactly the right amount of smarts to accomplish all that you will do while you're here. It's all perfect . . . and so are you!

To me, a person like my son-in-law Joe, who can lay a beautiful hardwood floor and have it come out flawlessly, is a genius. Whether or not he performed well in some aptitude test, Joe's genius is displayed in his artistic sense—in that magnificent mind that arranges and positions the grain of the wood, leveling and sealing, with endless measurements and computations. You too have all the intelligence you need for anything that ignites your creative and problem-solving passion. Believe this about yourself and you'll never want or need to trot out the excuse of *I'm not smart enough* again.

4. The Rules Won't Let Me

Always obeying the rules is a meme, or a mind virus that's become an acceptable indicator of your honesty and integrity. But note this sentence in a letter that Martin Luther King, Jr., wrote from the Birmingham city jail on April 16, 1963: "We can never forget that everything Hitler did in Germany was 'legal' and everything the Hungarian freedom fighters did in Hungary was 'illegal.'" I also love this observation from Ralph Waldo Emerson: "No law can be sacred to me but that of my nature."

I'm not making a case for being lawless and indifferent to edicts that govern a civilized society. I *am* encouraging you to recognize what some of our finest minds say about running your life by rules. I include here what my great teacher Lao-tzu wrote in the Tao Te Ching:

> *When the greatness of the Tao is present,*
> *action arises from one's own heart.*
> *When the greatness of the Tao is absent,*
> *action comes from the rules . . .*

Live your life in accordance with a Tao-centered or God-realized point of view. You know what is right, what your heart tells you. You know that you don't need cumbersome rules laid down by others, some of which make no sense to obey at all, to guide you. This fourth excuse is a huge cop-out in every sense of the word.

I want to cite one more famous American who was adamant about the need for feeling a sense of independence as a criterion for living a full, happy, successful, and healthy life. Read his words carefully: "The care of every man's soul belongs to himself. But what if he neglect[s] the care of it? Well, what if he neglect[s] the care of his health or estate . . . will the magistrate make a law that he shall not be poor or sick? Laws provide against injury from others; but not from ourselves. God himself will not save men against their wills." The person who wrote those words was none other than Thomas Jefferson.

So there you have some of history's most admired teachers reminding you that the rules should never be a final factor in determining anything about yourself. Instead, these wise men ask you to go within and be guided by what your passion dictates (as long as it doesn't hurt anyone else, of course).

If you have a tendency to employ the excuse *The rules won't let me,* know that it was handed down and enforced by those who wished to control your behavior. Yet here again, it's important to take full responsibility for your own actions. You're no longer a child who needs rules to make sure that you're safe, healthy, and functional within a family or a classroom. Be willing to consult your adult sense of what's right *for you.* Assertively pursue that vision, keeping a silent vigil on your inner passion. Overlook the pressures to do things by following instructions and edicts that are simply no longer applicable to you.

As you can see, all of these excuses originated in the earliest years of your life. But even as you take responsibility for your role in excuse making, always be kind to yourself. Remember that you only did what you knew how to do when you were a child. So go visit those "wrecks" Longfellow talks about in the quotation that begins this chapter—discover where they came from and why they've persisted for so long as your habituated ways of thinking. Do as the poet suggests and move on to an *Excuses Begone!* life, which is far more noble than an existence full of self-sabotaging explanations.

Suggestions for Applying the
Second Paradigm Question

— The most helpful suggestion I can offer you regarding the question of *Where did these excuses come from?* is to answer it with the following four words: *they came from me.* Take total responsibility for your thoughts in the form of the words that come out of your mouth today. By all means study the proliferation of mind viruses and early-childhood conditioning practices that were directed your way. But also practice thinking and saying this: *I chose to use excuses as a child. I didn't realize at the time that I had other choices available. I realize I've continued to choose those excuses until now.*

Be solely responsible—you have no one to blame. You don't need to wait for anyone to come around and undo what he or she did, since you can't become an excuse maker without giving your consent. And if you have given your consent, the *Excuses Begone!* paradigm revokes it now.

— Forgive everyone, including yourself. All those individuals who proliferated mind viruses and conditioning were only doing what they knew how to do given the circumstances of their lives, and those meme dispensers are only one generation removed from receiving the same kind of habituated thinking. Keep in mind the line from the Prayer of Saint Francis: "It is in pardoning that we are pardoned." Eschew blame and free yourself from anything that's been plaguing your life and holding you back from activating your highest calling. By forgiving everyone, you pardon them . . . and yourself. And remember, if you'd never blamed anyone for your tendencies toward being an excuse maker, you'd have no one to forgive!

THE THIRD QUESTION: *WHAT'S THE PAYOFF?*

"[W]e lie to ourselves, in order that we may still have the excuse of ignorance, the alibi of stupidity and incomprehension, possessing which we can continue with a good conscience to commit and tolerate the most monstrous crimes."

— Aldous Huxley

In the quotation above, from Huxley's essay "Words and Behavior," the "monstrous crimes" are committed by *and* against yourself, allowing you to continue habituated—and detrimental—thought patterns through dishonesty. This third question will help you clarify the psychological system that supports such lying.

Why maintain a thinking habit that impedes your highest vision for yourself? The solution seems easy enough: Simply stop using the excuses! But it obviously takes more than this to eliminate your mental crutches, otherwise you'd have abandoned them by now. It's similar to the alcoholic or drug addict who knows that his reasons for not quitting are holding him back, yet his behavior continues unabated. In some way you must feel that you're benefiting from your self-sabotaging thoughts, even when the facts indicate otherwise.

Your answer to *What's the payoff?* will give you insight into the reward system you've carefully constructed. It's the reason you can reach into your bag of excuses and pull out some real gems whenever it's convenient. And the fact that these thought patterns have been with you for most of your life makes them almost automatic responses.

Take a moment now to reflect on why your thoughts might sustain behaviors that don't serve your highest ideals. William Wordsworth, the insightful English poet, once remarked: "Habits rule the unreflecting herd," with *herd* being used as a pejorative term for thinking like everyone else. Your goal is to disrupt those habits that have led you to act like just one more member of the obedient pack, and that requires a new kind of understanding. Such understanding may be more accessible now than in the first part of your life, which was when you tended to form and accumulate your habits. Thoreau's words encourage you to make this second part of your life work for you by changing your path:

> As a single footstep will not make a path on the earth, so a single thought will not make a single pathway in the mind. To make a deep physical path, we walk again and again. To make a deep mental path, we must think over and over the kind of thoughts we wish to dominate our lives.

The *Excuses Begone!* paradigm invites you to explore the same kinds of reasoning that created your habit of excuse making, and then develop a new set of beliefs. Just as an elephant can be tethered by a thread if it believes that it's being held captive, if you believe that you're chained to your excuses, you're in bondage. Asking *What's the payoff?* allows you to gain insight into the nature of your servitude to old thought processes, and helps you form a new path in your mind that will soon become well worn.

For example, there was a time in my life when I consumed eight or more artificially sweetened soft drinks a day. My excuse was that I'd always done this, so it would be way too difficult to break the habit. Then I happened to read Epictetus's *Handbook of Conscious Living* (written by students from his oral teachings more than 2,000 years ago), and this passage jumped out at me: "Nothing is in reality either pleasant or unpleasant by nature; but all things become so by habit." This was a great insight for me. The junk I was drinking daily wasn't pleasurable because of what it was or how it tasted; it was simply something I'd done for so long that I'd worn a path in my brain from which I thought there was no escape.

In 1986, armed with this new insight and nothing more, I began to create a *new* path. I kept reminding myself that this artificially sweetened brown water wasn't pleasurable in and of itself—it was only my habit that made it so. To this day, I haven't even had a sip of any kind of soda. So as you can see, getting to the bottom of why we tread the same path day after day can be very helpful and life changing.

Common Hidden Payoffs for Excuse Making

I've used the word *hidden* to alert you to the fact that you're often totally unaware of the reasons why you continue to walk down the same path and rely on the same old excuses. Many behaviors and thought patterns persist because of perceived rewards . . . which may not be that good for you. In fact, most of the psychological benefits you receive from your excuse-making habit are actually quite self-destructive.

The most prevalent psychological payoffs used to support your nasty habits are discussed in the following pages. Apply the insights you acquire from reading about them to create a new excuse-free path within your own mind:

1. Avoidance

When you grab on to a self-sabotaging belief, it only serves to keep you marching in place. *It's going to be very difficult . . . It's going to take up way too much of my time . . . What I want is too big . . . I don't have the money . . .* and so on merely justify your inaction with an explanation. And once you've done so, you're free to enjoy the avoidance payoff.

I was a doctoral-student advisor at a major university for six years in the 1970s. I found that with very few exceptions, most doctoral students were able to complete the course work—but when it came time to write their dissertation (which is a very involved research project that's generally the length of a book and must be completed to earn a Ph.D.) and then defend it before a committee of faculty members, many of them fell short. They'd justify their behavior with *I'm too busy . . . I'm not smart enough to write and defend a book . . . It will take a long time . . . I don't have the energy . . .* and many more from the catalog of excuses. Such explanations were absolutely vital for those who were trying to avoid something.

Avoidance is a common and easily identifiable payoff, or the psychological reward that allows you to be somewhat at peace with yourself when you make self-thwarting decisions. The excuse becomes your ally, even though it's an ally that doesn't have your best interests at heart.

2. Safety

None of us like to feel unsafe, so excuses become what we use to avoid potentially dangerous situations. Rather than wandering off into uncharted territory where we might face the risk of low performance, failure, criticism, exhaustion, the unknown, appearing foolish, getting hurt, and the like, it's more convenient to retreat into a haven of familiarity. The problem is that the excuse habit only brings us a false sense of security, in the same way a "blanky" comforts a frightened child.

190

Inside you there's a powerful calling that's urging you to fulfill the destiny you feel churning through your veins, yet taking the safest route is causing you to avoid that calling. On the one hand, you feel pulled toward your purpose; and on the other, any number of convenient excuses sing to you like sirens. *It will be risky . . . It's not my nature . . . I'm too scared . . . There will be family drama . . . I'm too old . . . It's too big . . .* and statements like them can be very difficult to ignore.

This brings to mind my daughter Tracy, who ignored her own calling for years. She had a secure job as an executive, with good benefits, excellent pay, nice people to work with, a great location, and lots of other reasons that could have kept her there until she retired at some point down the road. Yet burning inside her was a strong desire to be her own boss, to use her design and marketing skills to create her own products. But when she talked about leaving her safe position with all of the benefits, she couldn't make the move, and her excuses provided her with the rationale she required.

After years of talking about why she couldn't follow her dream, my daughter finally decided to put the *Excuses Begone!* paradigm to work for her. Today she's the CEO of her own company, called Urban Junket. She designs high-quality women's handbags and laptop bags, traveling the world to procure the very best materials. While she hasn't attained her previous salary and benefits level yet, she's happy, fulfilled, and very pleased with what she has created. Tracy is no longer a slave to the payoff her excuses offered her. Check out her beautiful creations online (**www.urbanjunket .com**) and send her a note of appreciation if her story of leaving excuses behind inspires you—as it does me, her very proud father.

3. The Easy Way Out

Any excuse at all offers the bountiful reward of *the easy way out*. Let's face it, when you're confronted with a choice between doing something requiring effort and something that's effortless and easy, you're apt to pick the latter, even if it's not the choice that will actually lead to your objectives.

Your highest self wants you to fulfill your destiny, which often involves some type of sacrifice, expenditure of time, mental and physical energy, and material resources. Ego is frequently in conflict with what your highest self desires—your false self pushes and cajoles you into staying put, threatened by anything that disrupts its mission of keeping you nice and comfortable by avoiding difficult choices. Thus, there's a big payoff for using excuses that allow you to take the easy road.

I know the effort and daily struggle I'm in for when I opt to sit and write, day in and day out, often for an entire year, until I complete a book. I've done it long enough to know with sweet certainty that the project's completion is fully aligned with my life's purpose. I recognize that sitting here in solitude and doing the work keeps me in balance, or aligned with the highest callings of my soul. Even so, over the years I've noticed the intense temptation to allow excuses to keep me from doing what my heart tells me I must. They insist: *It's too big a project, and you don't have the energy. You don't have anything else to prove, so just relax. You're tired—let up on yourself. Writing takes you away from your family, and you're already overcommitted.*

These statements and others like them would give me an easy payoff if I allowed them to. I could then avoid the anxiety, struggle, loneliness, and nose-to-the-grindstone actions that are a necessary part of the creative process. But there's far more joy when I see the results of my labors, along with all the good such efforts seem to be doing in the world, than any temporary pleasure I might gain by taking the easy way out and avoiding what I know I need to do.

4. Manipulation

One of the great payoffs that so many of these excuses provide is the opportunity to manipulate others into doing your bidding.

While this may not be seen as the most positive of things, that's nevertheless just what happens. When you make the choice to use an excuse such as *I don't have the energy . . . I'm too busy . . . I'm not strong enough or smart enough . . .* or the like, you place the responsibility on some other person. After you've given that person your explanations for why you can't do something, you can then sit back comfortably and watch how they spur him or her into action.

As the father of eight children, I've seen this strategy thousands of times. For example:

— *I'm too tired* translates to: *Have someone else do the chore.* The payoff? *I get to sleep while another person takes over my responsibilities.*

— *I can't afford it* or *I spent all my money* translates to: <u>*You*</u> *buy what I want or need.* The payoff? *I've manipulated you with my generic excuse.*

— *I don't deserve it* translates to: *Feel sorry for me.* The payoff? *You're going to give me what I want because you can't stand to see me feeling unworthy.*

Of course you don't have to be a child in a family to benefit from virtually all of these excuses that, in one way or another, allow you to manipulate others into doing your bidding.

5. Being Right

There's nothing that the false self loves more than being right—and making someone else wrong—and excuses are tailor-made for this. When you use an excuse, you get to feel superior and put someone else in the position of being a loser . . . and ego loves feeling like a winner, especially at the expense of others.

Excuses are simply explanations you make to yourself that have no necessary bearing on the truth—yet even though they're lies, they do bring you some sort of reward. So while your only evidence may be a habitual thought, if you convince yourself that you're right, you get to retreat into the illusion of winning. In this case, the excuse is a deception that props up your low self-esteem. You've substituted an excuse in place of authentic self-worth, and the payoff is that your reasoning helps you live with yourself without acknowledging your self-deceit.

So:

— *No one will ever help me* translates to: *I'm not deserving or lucky enough to get others to help me, just like I've always said. So there you have it—I'm right again.*

— *The rules won't let me* translates to: *See how smart I am? I've always said that you can't get ahead, and anyone who disagrees with me is a loser.*

— *There will be family drama* translates to: *I'm right about this family, and I've always been right. All the rest of you just don't know as much as I do.*

On and on goes this convoluted logic. When you're an excuse maker, you need to be right and haul out anything you can think of to prove to the world how wrong it is. And, conversely, how right you are!

6. Blame

When you resort to using an excuse, the ultimate payoff is that you remove responsibility for your own shortcomings and place responsibility for them on the shoulders of someone else. I've written about this blame game throughout this book: once again, this is the work of the ego, that false self that doesn't believe in your infinite Divine nature but does keep track of how well you stack up against the people and events of this material world.

If you're not doing well, the ego says that it's someone else's fault. If you're *unhappy, unhealthy, indigent, unlucky, fearful,* or any other negative descriptor that you can come up with, this is all the fault of something or someone external to yourself. While your highest self happily thrives on humility, the ego is exceptionally proud. Thus, when anything goes wrong, the ego's inclination is to blame someone else and maintain its pride.

Blame pays a colossal dividend, so the ego constructs something to bring it about whenever possible. That's why when you blame the economy, the political party in power, the oil-rich sheiks in Saudi Arabia, or anyone else you can think of, your false self receives a reward. Unable to save money, get investors for your pet project, pay your bills, or justify your bankruptcy? Not only does the blame game provide you with a convenient scapegoat, but it also delivers a rich payoff for continuing to use all of the excuses that have become a way of life.

7. Protection

When you were a child, you were most likely offered the protection of your family. You were small; they were big. You didn't have much; they controlled just about everything. You had to ask permission; they doled out their authority. In other words, you were protected. As you grew into adulthood, these leftover behaviors were convenient to hang on to, even though being grown meant no longer seeking permission from parents or getting the sustenance you had when you were little. A host of excuses evolved that had the feeling of being protected as their primary payoff, so you may still be thinking and acting like a kid.

To maintain the benefits of childhood without appearing childish, you've created excuses that allow you to retreat into the familiar territory of feeling taken care of. Reasons why you're not manifesting the life you desire provide you with the reward of being able to retreat to the feeling of being a little boy or girl again. This is a powerful payoff indeed, even though it doesn't serve you very well as an adult.

As a parent, I've felt that my job isn't to be someone my children can lean on, but rather to help them realize that leaning is unnecessary. As some of my kids reached adulthood, however, I noted that they were obviously reluctant to take on the full mantle of self-responsibility. As excuses surfaced, I saw that they were seeking the protection of having everything decided for them. *I'm not strong enough* translated to: *You do it for me, Daddy, and then I can feel protected again.* And *I can't afford it* translated to: *You pay for it, and then I'm off the hook.*

Similarly, so many of the excuses you may be using have that built-in dividend of allowing you to explain away your deficiencies and feel like a protected youngster again. While regressing back to childhood may let you feel temporarily protected, it's obviously going to keep you stuck in place—after all, reality dictates that Mommy and Daddy cannot shield you ad infinitum.

8. Escaping the Present Moment

The now is all there is. It is all that has ever been and all that will ever be. Yet just as there are many ways to live gloriously and happily in the present moment, there are also many ways to attempt to escape from living fully in the now. And that's where excuses come in.

Like all other mental activities, excuse making takes place totally in the here-and-now. When you engage in this practice, that's how you use up the present. If you're devoting the moment to justification and defensiveness, then it isn't possible to use it to do something constructive, work at changing, make love, marvel at your children, enjoy each breath you take, and so forth. The payoff is that you get something to do with your time. Even though it may be neurotic in nature, it's nevertheless a convenient escape mechanism to keep you stuck in your old habits.

The present is all you'll ever have, and every excuse you use keeps you from being here now. While you can never avoid the now, excuse making makes certain that you won't change old habits, since you'll be too busy filling up your precious seconds with excuses.

Suggestions for Reversing These Payoffs

Now let's turn the eight payoffs around and see how they can work for you rather than against you. Read these suggestions with the intention of outgrowing old thinking habits, as well as discovering the harmony of living from your highest vision:

1. Avoidance

Make the decision that you'll no longer use excuses to keep you from what you know is in your best interest. Today, act on something you've always avoided and explained away with a convenient excuse. Make that phone call you've been putting off, write a letter to a distant friend or relative, put on a pair of walking shoes and go on a one-mile jaunt, clean out one section of your closet—do anything at all, as long as it's something you've been justifying not doing with excuses.

Affirm: *I have a free will, and there is nothing I need to avoid. I will refrain from using any excuses to justify my avoidance behavior.*

2. Safety

Plan to take a vacation without any guarantees—just go, and let yourself be guided by your instincts rather than a detailed itinerary. Eat at a restaurant that serves food you're unfamiliar with, attend a symphony or a soccer game, visit a mosque, take a yoga class, go on a nature hike, or do anything else that you may have been afraid of. Decide to outgrow the excuses you've employed, and adopt a philosophy of having a mind that's open to everything and attached to nothing.

Affirm: *I choose the less-traveled path and resist seeking out familiarity and an illusion of security.*

3. The Easy Way Out

Have a conversation with your subconscious mind, which has grown accustomed to choosing the familiar path, and explain that you're no longer interested in living in this way. Then go into reversal mode: rather than congratulating yourself for avoiding something difficult, cheer yourself on for having the courage and the determination to move in a new and possibly uncomfortable direction.

At one time, my payoff system for a self-defeating smoking habit was the belief that *I receive pleasure from this activity, so I'm not going to quit.* Clearly, my mind felt that continuing this filthy habit was far easier than quitting. But after many conversations with my subconscious mind, the day came when I reversed my reward system. Instead of using my old payoff procedure, I began to congratulate myself for having the internal strength to make the difficult choice rather than the familiar and easy one.

Affirm: *I am open to making difficult choices when they happen to be in harmony with my highest good.*

4. Manipulation

Have a conversation with yourself *before* you speak or act in a way that's likely to cause you to manipulate others. A private inner dialogue is crucial in eliminating this old psychological payoff system that you've inadvertently created. When it comes to your family members and close friends, also have these silent conversations—no one need know what you're doing. With your children, for instance, practice noninterference and remind yourself that in most cases, they already know what to do.

Weigh what the consequence is likely to be if you were to say a particular thing. Anticipate how others in the room might react, how you'd respond, and what might flare up. (All of this will only take a second or two.) The end result may be that you simply stay silent and allow your ego to take a well-deserved break, rather than doling out advice that is really a form of manipulation.

Affirm: *I am content within myself. I have no need to control or manipulate anyone so that they will think and act as I prefer.*

5. Being Right

The ego spends a lot of time practicing always being right. In order to remove this item from your psychological portfolio, begin letting *others* be right. When someone says something that you'd normally disagree with for the purpose of making them wrong, try saying, "You're right about that." This will immediately put a reverse spin on the ego's need to be right.

If someone tells you, "You always ignore my point of view, and we end up doing what you want," try this reply on for size: "You know, that's really a good point that I've never considered before. The more I think about what you're saying to me, the more I realize that you're right about that." *Voilà*—the cycle of arguing stops, the psychological support system for using excuses is reversed, and you begin a conflict-free life!

Make these words the cornerstone of your new policy by repeating them to others as often as possible: *You're right about that.* While the ego will loudly protest, this strategy can only bring you peace and happiness. So would you rather be right or happy?

Affirm: *I release the inclination to make anyone else wrong.*

6. Blame

Remind yourself that no one can ever make you feel anything without your consent. Therefore, there's no one to blame for whatever is taking place in your life. With this simple concept, you permanently eliminate the payoff system of blaming others for your shortcomings, and eradicate a tendency toward excuse making.

Tell yourself: *I am the sum total of all of the choices I've made in my life, even those I made as a small child.* When your ego launches into its blame game with *It's not my fault . . . I couldn't help it . . . They made me do it . . .* and so on, stay firm about your choice to begin abolishing payoffs with the *Excuses Begone!* guide.

Affirm: *I practice self-responsibility rather than faultfinding, and I am willing to forgo the inclination to blame others for anything in my life.*

7. Protection

The words of Johann van Goethe may help you release the desire to seek the protection of childhood: "If children grew up according to early indications, we should have nothing but geniuses." And, from the great Indian poet Rabindranath Tagore: "Every child comes with the message that God is not yet discouraged of man." Goethe and Tagore are saying that you're someone who came here to fulfill a personal dharma, so let that genius gift from God finally be active in your life.

Everything you need to fulfill your destiny was with you at the moment before, during, and after your conception—so retreat to that knowledge now. Your payoff system of feeling fragile and needy and wanting to be protected dissolves as you begin to trust yourself. At the same time, you're trusting in the infinite wisdom that created you.

Affirm: *I am a grown-up, and I arrived here from nonbeing equipped with everything I need to fulfill my greatness.*

8. Escaping the Present Moment

When you feel dejected or out of sorts, ask yourself: *Do I wish to use the present moment—the precious currency of my life—in this manner?* This will help you to become conscious of the importance of being here now—not just in your body, but in your thinking as well. I urge you to think of the present as just that: a wondrous present from your Source. Anytime you're filling the now with thoughts about how you used to be, concerns about what someone has done to harm you, or worries about the future, you're saying "No, thank you" to your Source for this precious gift.

As I've pointed out throughout this book, everything that has ever happened did so not in the past, but in the now—so your relationship to life is your relationship to the now. Become conscious of just how valuable this present is, and obliterate that old tendency to use excuses for the purpose of escaping the moment.

Affirm: *I refuse to use my precious present moments in any way that takes me away from the Divine love from which I originated.*

This concludes the third question of the *Excuses Begone!* paradigm. Do you see the folly of your self-paralyzing excuses mentality? As you close out this chapter and move on to the next one, ponder these poetic words from Walt Whitman's *Leaves of Grass:*

> *There was a child went forth every day,*
> *And the first object he looked upon and received with*
> *wonder or pity or love or dread, that object he became,*
> *And that object became part of him for the*
> *day or a certain part of the day . . .*
> *or for many years or stretching cycles of years.*

So watch what you look upon. Even more significantly, don't create a reward system of excuses to defend, pity, or dread. This is a great time to remember this thought, which I frequently repeat: *When you change the way you look at things, the things you look at change.*

CHAPTER 15

THE FOURTH QUESTION: *WHAT WOULD MY LIFE LOOK LIKE IF I COULDN'T USE THESE EXCUSES?*

"What is now proved was once only imagin'd."
— William Blake

In the fourth question of the *Excuses Begone!* paradigm, you switch into the powerful world of your own imagination. The observation above, from the English poet William Blake, reveals an important truth: the things that you take for granted and treat as gospel were initially imagined. Just as the cell phone had to first be an idea before it became a reality, the same is true of everything you encounter in life.

Imagination is crucial in order to bring things from the world of nonbeing into the world of being. Jesus of Nazareth said that it's the Spirit that gives life, and Lao-tzu said that all being comes from nonbeing. What was good enough for these two spiritual giants to embrace has immeasurable importance for you as well.

This pathway from nonbeing or Spirit to the world of an *Excuses Begone!* existence originates in your imagination. I love to remind myself of this mind-blowing idea that I touched upon in Chapter 11: *An infinity of forests lies dormant within the dreams of one acorn.* Even a forest needs a vision, a dream, an idea; indeed, a fertile imagination.

This chapter is designed to help you do the same kind of work as one little acorn, which has an entire forest to create. You have within you the power to create a series of ideas for yourself that will erase obstacles to your highest calling. When you imagine that you're free of any need to use excuses, you'll ultimately act on what you're imagining. So practice the process of envisioning precisely what your life would look and feel like if it were impossible to enlist your excuse patterns. A good way to begin is by getting accustomed to visualizing exactly who you are, *as if you've already arrived.*

Seeing Who You Want to Be as Already Here

Let's look further at the quote that opens this chapter, along with the implications of breaking our excuse-making habit. Our poet friend Mr. Blake is saying that we imagined these self-limiting ideas before they became facts in our life. Memetics, genetics, early-childhood reinforcements, cultural conditioning, and years of thinking limiting thoughts joined forces to become the excuses that have come to feel like reality.

If Blake's observation is true for you, its corollary applies as well. In other words, if you make the *Excuses Begone!* shift and hold fast to its ideas, then you prove to yourself just how powerful your imagination is. This is why I included the words *already here* concerning the way you want to see yourself. For all intents and purposes, what you actively imagine is authentically and undeniably already here, so you can absolutely change from self-defeating excuses to self-enhancing actions. Once your new thinking habits are truly in place, it's the same as saying that you're already actualizing what you want.

When I was in my early 20s, I used the imagination practice on the excuse *I'm too tired.* I'd heard this so frequently that it finally became a mind virus I mimicked and employed regularly. It was a convenient but debilitating excuse, because thinking and talking about how tired I was made me more fatigued than I actually was. The more I said the words *I'm tired,* the more my energy seemed to be depleted, even when there were no physical reasons behind this.

One morning after listening to a friend tell me that he was too exhausted to carry out a planned weekend retreat, I decided to end my use of this excuse permanently. I pledged to never again tell others (or myself) how tired I was, and I began to imagine myself in possession of unlimited energy. I didn't change my sleep habits, take energy supplements, or change my lifestyle—all I did was imagine myself as a high-energy person. I was able to change the way I viewed myself in relationship to fatigue and started to see myself as a never-tired person. This all started with a new thought, which was placed first in my imagination. And to this day, some 40 years later, I've steadfastly refused to even think *I'm tired.*

One of Ralph Waldo Emerson's essays includes a line that has always made an impact on me: "Imagination is a very high sort of seeing." To me, this is seeing with a capital *S*. Seeing myself with boundless energy all those years ago allowed me to eliminate the obstacles of fatigue and energy depletion, and I created a new me in those imaginative moments.

Imagining Your Way to a Life Without Excuses

I encourage you to actively examine the question *What would my life look like if I couldn't use these excuses?* by giving yourself permission to let your imagination run wild. Envision something like a magical potion that doesn't permit you to think thoughts that have anything to do with excuses, and pay attention to what this visualization provokes within you. What would life look like? How would you feel? What alternative thoughts would you have?

I'll take you through this exercise now, using several of the excuses from the 18-item catalog I detailed in Chapter 3:

1. It Will Be Difficult/It Will Take a Long Time

These two similar excuses are frequently substituted for action. Now, imagine that you're incapable of creating these thoughts. In the same way that you can't imagine the mental activity of a jelly-fish without ears or eyes that lives in the middle of the sea, neither can you conceive of a task as being difficult or taking a long time. So if it were absolutely impossible for you to think this way, what would your life be like?

Whatever it is that you'd like to accomplish, be it becoming an artist, creating your own musical composition, starting a new business, repairing your relationship with your parents or spouse or anyone else, building a new home, getting into physical shape—anything at all—how would your world change if you couldn't even conceive of the idea that it would be difficult and/or take a long time?

— **Without these excuses, what would life look like?** It's a safe bet that you'd immediately initiate action propelling you in the direction of the fulfillment of your dreams. You'd talk to others who had similar kinds of dreams and then emerged successfully. You'd have a lot of energy, and you'd be actively engaged in the process of living the life you imagine. You'd attract synchronistic assistance and notice the right people, the right events, and the right circumstances persistently showing up. Why? Because you'd be acting just like the Source of all creation does. You'd be aligned with a universe that says, "Yes, you can!" and gives you the tools to prove it. You'd have no hesitation or fear that something would be difficult or take too long . . . you'd happily *do* rather than explain or complain.

— **Without these excuses, how would you feel?** With these limitations completely out of the way, let me hazard a guess that you'd feel ecstatic and finally, completely on purpose. A sense of freedom would delight you, because avoidance of your true dharma would no longer exist. You'd feel enormous contentment rather than worrying about what you're avoiding or where you're going. There would be no focus on your destination since *too long* would no longer exist for you, and the *now* of the journey would provide the success and happiness you desire. You'd experience a great deal of bliss because you'd be guided by your creativity and initiative rather than fear of disappointment, and joy would rule your life.

— Without these excuses, what alternative thoughts would you have? Rather than focusing on what you can't do because it's difficult and takes a long time, you'd think like this: *This is definitely something that I can and will create for myself. I know I can do anything I put my mind to. I anticipate that this is within my ability to readily accomplish. I have no fear, because I recognize that whatever guidance and assistance I require is available. I'm excited, thrilled, and elated about fulfilling this dream. I realize that the thoughts I have are meshed with enthusiasm and passion, and that nothing can stop me. In fact, I'm certain that whatever I need to actualize my dreams is already on its way. I contentedly watch for what the universe sends me.*

2. There Will Be Family Drama

Again, I'm suggesting that you see yourself as utterly incapable of coming up with this excuse. Imagine that you can't conjure up even a single thought that forecasts any kind of familial disruption. Thinking in this way is equivalent to anticipating that your relatives are fine with whatever decision you make—you absolutely will not experience resistance, criticism, hostility, or rejection. Your family is, at the very least, neutral and perhaps even indifferent. There are no hassles or antagonisms, and no drama for you to deal with.

— Without this excuse, what would life look like? Since you'd no longer have to consider the ramifications of your family knowing the authentic you, your life would be exactly how you always wanted it to be. You'd never have to consult anyone whose opinion you didn't value: you'd choose the kind of work you prefer, study the subjects you wished to, live where you pleased, and come and go as you determined—without a single moment of conflict or disapproval from your relatives. Disproving the popular saying that "friends are God's way of apologizing for our relatives," your family members would even become your close friends!

— **Without this excuse, how would you feel?** You'd feel free, because now drama could never be a consequence of following your bliss.

Take a second now to imagine your family enthusiastically encouraging every decision that you make concerning your life . . . this is how you'd feel every day if it was impossible to entertain the thoughts that are the basis of this excuse. With everyone around you at peace, you'd feel the soothing effect of a harmonious and supportive environment. Anxiety and worry would disappear, and you'd feel in charge of your inner world, perhaps for the first time. Feeling safe would replace all the fear of potential condemnation that forced you to behave like such a good little family member.

— **Without this excuse, what alternative thoughts would you have?** Your new thoughts would be based exclusively on the best way to conduct your life, since you wouldn't be able to employ the family-drama excuse. You'd think: *I'm in a position to ask anyone I love for his or her opinion, and I can accept or reject that advice without any negative repercussions coming my way. I'm free to practice any religion I choose, or none at all. I'm free to date, marry, or cohabit with whomever I choose. I'm free to pursue any line of work, live in any location, and just plain live my life, and all of my family members love me and support my choices.*

This doesn't need to be a fantasy—it's your mind, and you have the freedom to fill it with the thoughts you choose. This new way of thinking is immediately available to you, just as soon as you do an *Excuses Begone!* makeover on this old belief.

3. I'm Not Strong Enough/I'm Not Smart Enough

What if you couldn't have these excuses? If you were incapable of believing that you're deficient physically and intellectually, you'd focus on the opposite idea. You'd think thoughts like the following, which reflect a new mind-set: *I'm as strong as I need to be to accomplish anything I place my attention on. I'm a creative genius, a piece of the Divine creator; therefore, I have in my possession all of the brainpower that I'll ever need to fulfill any desires of my choosing.*

Before you object to these lofty self-pronouncements, remind yourself that the point of this exercise is to help you imagine a new existence without your old mental crutches.

— **Without these excuses, what would life look like?** Here again, you'd bask in the exquisite belief that you possess all of the physical and intellectual abilities you could ever need. Your life would flow naturally from a position of supreme confidence in yourself and all of your God-given, natural abilities. You'd take risks and be capable of trying anything, content with whatever results were to ensue. You'd exude courage because you'd be unable to manufacture doubtful thoughts that manifested as excuses. You'd never compare yourself to others or evaluate your abilities on the basis of what others do—how you measure up to the performance levels of others would have no bearing on you or what you attempt. You'd know that God doesn't make mistakes, so whatever levels of personal strength and intellectual proficiency you possess are absolutely perfect. In short, you'd be content, grateful for who you are and all that you'd been given, in both the physical and perceptual realms.

— **Without these excuses, how would you feel?** The most noticeable feelings you'd experience would be self-assurance and personal pride. You'd have a sense of bliss stemming from being completely satisfied with who you are. You'd feel awe and pleasure about the miracle of your mind and body. You'd no longer cast your gaze outward and feel inadequate by comparison; instead, you'd look inward and feel peaceful and blessed, independent of the opinion of others.

— Without these excuses, what alternative thoughts would you have? With no more excuses about mental and physical inadequacies, you'd engage in all kinds of new and nourishing beliefs. Your first one might be something like this: *I have all the mental and physical tools I need to actualize any dream I've ever had. All I need to do is maintain my passion, and all of the assistance I need will come to me.*

Without excuses, there wouldn't be any way of creating obstacles for yourself. But just thinking *I am strong* or *I am smart* begins to stop the excuse-making modes in their tracks. With the positive attitude of *I can do it; I have all that I need right here and right now,* you're on the way to fulfilling the destiny that was in that tiny little embryo that became *you.* That little embryo knew nothing of limitations, weaknesses, stupidity, and the like. It had a Divine nature; it was perfect; and it had everything it needed in the way of mental and material strength to fulfill the destiny that it signed up to accomplish.

Once the excuses are gone, there will be nothing to stop you from thinking and acting in harmony with the gifts that you were given at the moment of your transition from nonbeing to being, from Spirit to form, from *no where* to *now here.*

4. I Don't Have the Energy/I'm Too Busy

Once again, remember to play with your imagination. You're imagining that your brain is constructed in such a way that there's no excuse-making apparatus. So the moment you contemplate pursuing something you've always wanted to accomplish, your thoughts center around the idea that you possess boundless energy to do anything you put your mind to, and that you have plenty of time to pursue these activities.

— Without these excuses, what would life look like? Life would have a high-energy appearance, and you'd enjoy thinking about accomplishing the things you've dreamed about. You might tell yourself: *I'm a vigorous person and possess all the vitality and liveliness to accomplish anything I set my mind to.* And with only this type of sentiment available, that's precisely the kind of action you'd take. Such an attitude would spur you on, giving you unlimited vim and vigor. You'd find joy in doing the kinds of things you always wanted to do but couldn't when you used to claim that you didn't have any energy or you were too busy.

Without those lame excuses, your life would shift from unmotivated to engaged in the daily activities that bring you a sense of well-being. Although you'd be busier than you ever were before, you wouldn't be thinking about business and crammed schedules as excuses for not living life totally on your own terms. You'd revel in knowing that your activities serve you in the best way because they're aligned with your highest aspirations for yourself.

— Without these excuses, how would you feel? You'd feel fully *alive, joyful, blissful,* and other similar happiness descriptors. But more than this, you'd notice a significant decline in the bodily sensations of fatigue, headaches, cramps, high blood pressure, coughing, congestion, fever, being overweight and out of breath, and other symptoms. That's because when you engage in activities that make you feel good, your body reacts with sensations of well-being—since you can't use an excuse to escape or explain away your desire to live your life on purpose, you enjoy optimal health. This is the equivalent of feeling the presence of your Source energy, which knows exactly why you're here and cooperates as soon as you become aligned with the energy that intended you here in the first place.

— Without these excuses, what alternative thoughts would you have? Imagine not being able to come up with the ideas that make up the foundation for these excuses. What would this leave as an alternative? You'd think: *I have all the juice and vitality I need* *for fulfilling my own dharma; I am highly energized. I trust in the wisdom of the Source in which I originated to provide me with all I need to match the grand design I have for my life. The very fact that I possess the passion for what I wish to accomplish means that I have the necessary high energy that is required.*

As you know, your actions flow directly from your thoughts. So if you couldn't come up with excuses to explain a lack of energy or an overly busy life, your thoughts would focus on what *is* possible rather than what *is not*. You'd muse about whatever brought you joy and kept you in harmony with your highest vision for yourself. You'd love having a full life, yet you'd happily eliminate activities that came under the heading of "busywork"—you wouldn't fill your days with drudgery or meaningless activities.

This is the way you think when you're unable to conjure up excuses.

Victor Hugo once made an observation that succinctly and emphatically sums up the message that I've attempted to convey in this fourth question of the *Excuses Begone!* paradigm: "One can resist the invasion of armies; one cannot resist the invasion of ideas." To that end, treat this exercise on imagination as the welcome arrival of a new idea. I've found it to be so powerful that in just a few brief applications, I've been able to permanently banish many excuses I once relied on.

If you're about to blame someone else for why your life isn't unfolding in the way you prefer, I encourage you to think about how your world would change if you didn't have the capacity to blame. Ask yourself the questions brought up in this chapter: *What would my life look like? How would I feel? What alternative thinking would I engage in, since my brain couldn't process any kind of excuse making, which lays the blame on anyone other than myself?*

Yes, that's it: you'd immediately turn to yourself. You wouldn't solve your problem; you'd simply outgrow it. That's the purpose of this paradigm, this chapter, and this entire book—grow up and live an *Excuses Begone!* life. When you integrate this concept, you welcome these new ideas into your life.

CHAPTER 16

THE FIFTH QUESTION: *CAN I CREATE A RATIONAL REASON TO CHANGE?*

"[N]either believe nor reject any thing because any other
person, or description of persons have rejected or believed it.
Your own reason is the only oracle given you by heaven . . ."

— Thomas Jefferson

My 21-year-old son, Sands, has a long-standing habit of being unable to wake up for his morning classes, and on weekends often sleeps until two in the afternoon. I've had countless discussions with him about breaking this habit, because he's continually dealing with tardiness issues in school, rushing around in the morning in a state of anxiety, driving fast because he's late, and being tired all day because of an insufficient amount of the precious sleep that his body seems to crave. His habit gets in the way of his schoolwork, his happiness, and his health, since he feels fatigued throughout any day in which he has to wake up before noon.

Whenever we discuss breaking this habit, my son's answers go like this: "I can't just change and jump up in the morning," "I've always been this way; it's my nature," "I don't have energy in the morning," "I'm young, and this is the way all my friends live," "I've tried, but it's never been something I can do," and "It's just too difficult." Sound familiar? Like most of us, my son has allowed his life to be ruled by excuses.

Four Criteria for Creating a Rational Reason to Change

The previous four questions in the *Excuses Begone!* paradigm urged you to examine whether your excuses are true, to look at their origins, to review the payoff system, and then to imagine what your life would look like if you were unable to even come up with these limiting thought patterns. What's needed now is to understand the necessity of using logic as you make a portentous shift in your life, which brings us to the fifth question: *Can I create a rational reason to change?*

If your desire to break any habit isn't matched by a reasoning process that *registers with you,* then your work in this new paradigm will be weakened to the point of ineffectiveness. So when you intellectually accept the four criteria below, your ability to undermine and undercut your old habituated patterns will have a solid base from which to proceed, and you'll graduate with honors from this complete course in *Excuses Begone!*

Criterion #1: It Must Make Sense

Eliminating lifelong thinking habits cannot and will not happen if it doesn't strike you as a sensible thing to do. It doesn't really matter that everyone you know tells you how important it is to change—if it doesn't make sense to you, then you'll retreat to your old ways and continue to explain them away with your convenient laundry list of excuses. If the answer to *Do I really want to bring about this change?* is yes, then that's all you need in order to proceed and succeed. But if you have any doubts whatsoever, your old excuse making will surface, and you'll revert back to your long-held habits.

For example, when I was in my 30s, I made the decision that I was no longer going to allow myself to continue the unhealthy habits that had dominated my life up until that point. I could see myself gaining weight around the middle, eating and drinking things that weren't good for me, and generally not paying the proper attention to the well-being of this temple that temporarily houses my soul. I remember thinking: *I'm going to change. I don't know how, but I do know that I can't rely on anyone else but myself. I'm not going to enter the afternoon of my life as an obese, out-of-breath, toxic man. It makes sense to me to make this shift, so that's what I'm going to stick with.*

One day in 1976, I began a regimen that included exercise, drinking lots of water, taking supplements, and improving my diet. Although no one around me fully understood my drive to stay in shape, it made sense to me. Consequently, I was able to begin a new strategy for living that resulted in eliminating all of those tired excuses I'd been using to explain my retreat from well-being.

Whenever anyone has told me over the years that they just don't understand why I'm so "compulsive" about my health habits, I always think: *If I didn't have a healthy body, I wouldn't have anywhere to live.* Because my lifestyle makes sense to me, I'm immune to others' perplexed questioning, and I'm never tempted to reverse my decision to live as healthful an existence as I possibly can. My rational determination to pursue optimal wellness makes self-defeating choices unappealing.

Today, I enjoy noticing the long-term effects of that decision I made more than three decades ago. Simply resolving to become more health conscious led me to run daily, which led me to eliminate red meat from my diet, which led me to drink water instead of alcohol, which led me to give up all soft drinks, which led me to swim regularly, which led me to eat more and more raw vegetables, which led me to practice Bikram yoga four to five times a week, which led me to study and live the Tao Te Ching . . . and on and on it goes.

Most obese persons know that their self-destructive patterns have brought them to more poor choices (explained away by excuses), until the final result is out of their control. And while all addicts started out small and gained one ruinous habit after another, *you* can choose to be someone who breaks free of limitations right now. This one basic thought: *This makes sense to me—even if no one else understands me and I don't know how to make it happen—and that's what I'm going to stick with,* will lead you to a new path to walk upon. Each step from that new position leads to another and then another, until you finally have the freedom that comes from living without the hindrance of excuses.

Criterion #2: It Must Be Doable

Within you is a private space where "no visitors are allowed." This is where you meet yourself in total honesty, where you know what you're willing to dream, desire, and ultimately do. It's also where you find your answer to this question: *Am I willing and able to do what it takes to overcome these long-held habits of thought and action?*

If the answer is that you just can't make a change—you know yourself well enough to predict that you won't do the work that's necessary to accomplish it—then you're wise to heed that response. Forget about changing those old habits, at least for now. However, if you don't know how you'll do it but you still feel that it's doable, then proceed. You'll find the answers coming to you because of your willingness to view these changes as a real possibility.

Here are a couple of examples from my life that occurred recently, at my tender age of 68:

— I attended a meeting with several television executives to discuss the possibility of hosting my own national show. The idea of spreading the word of higher consciousness and promoting a loving, compassionate approach to helping people appealed to me. I've been doing precisely that on my radio show each

Monday on **HayHouseRadio.com®** for the past few years, so the thought of expanding this to a much larger audience was indeed tempting.

But in that honest place within me, where the NO VISITORS ALLOWED sign hangs, I found hosting a national TV show to simply not be doable. It's not about having excuses; it's about the fact that I'm just not willing to give up my writing, yoga practice, ocean swimming, long walks, hikes in the woods, or time with those I love. Because it's not going to happen and I know this, I simply let it go, with no excuses necessary for my decision. It's not doable, period. No complaining; no explaining.

— The second example involved a totally new experience that would take me all the way out of my comfort zone. It would be an opportunity to test myself in such a way that would be highly challenging, requiring me to have the mettle to overcome some old habits that had been supported by excuses. I was asked to be in a full-length motion picture based on the teachings that I've been associated with throughout my professional career.

Even though I was to play myself in a script that included professional actors, this endeavor would still require me to take direction from a well-established film director, learn lines, shoot scenes over and over and over from every conceivable angle, and work on a movie set for a month. It would entail 12-hour days; often staying up all night and working outdoors; and always being told what to do, where to sit, how to react, where to go next, what to wear, and on and on. These experiences were certainly foreign to all that I've done in the past three-plus decades . . . but it was doable for me. In that quiet, private place within me, I was thrilled at the idea of learning to become an actor in a movie based upon my teachings.

Once I knew that this project had an inner *go,* I totally surrendered to the process. I knew that the greater good would be served by the film, and I let go of all of my reasons (excuses) for not taking it on: *I know it will be difficult. It's a real risk. I've never acted before. I don't take direction. I do what I want, when I want, and*

I say what I'm guided to say. It's not my nature to be an actor. No one will help me; I'll be hopelessly lost. I've never done such a thing before—what if I look stupid? I'm too old to learn a new profession, let alone master it, at the age of 68. A movie is too big a project. I'm too busy with my writing and overly full schedule. I'm scared—I don't like being put in a position where I might look bad, or even worse, fail!

And so I arrived on the set to meet the director, actors, sound and lighting people, and rehearsal folks with a new attitude. I came ready to listen, learn, and master whatever skills I needed to create this full-length movie. Once I knew that it made sense and was definitely doable (even though I didn't have a clue as to how I'd accomplish it), all that I needed (and much more) began to show up right on time. The moment I stowed my skepticism, every excuse for not being involved in the project disappeared.

I must add here that I met some of the most intriguing people I've ever known, all of whom have become close friends. I loved the entire experience, and there's now a beautiful motion picture thanks to the accomplished actors, director, editors, and film crew. Titled *The Shift*, it brings me more pride and joy than I can describe.

Criterion #3: It Must Allow You to Feel Good

Your left brain deals with the details of your life—this is where you analyze, compute, figure, and get all of your ducks in a row—and the first two criteria detailed above speak right to it. When you ask yourself the question *Can I create a rational reason to change?* your intellect responds: *Yes, indeed, that does make sense, and I really believe that I can do this thing and bring about the desired changes.*

Your right brain, on the other hand, deals with things like your emotions, your intuition, your enthusiasm, your awareness, and even your consciousness. So let's examine the creation of a rational reason to change from the right brain's point of view and discover how this change *feels*.

When I did this exercise in connection with the possibility of having my own daily TV program, I didn't feel good at all. I felt tense, rushed, tight in my stomach, and nervous about all of the time I'd have to devote to the show. I actually began to feel sick, and that was enough for me. My emotions, which show up in my body as a result of my thoughts, were giving me the answer. Contrast this with what happened when I visualized how I'd feel after taking up the movie/acting challenge: I felt dizzy with excitement about learning a completely new craft—not to mention strong, content, and proud. My emotions actually empowered me.

If you want to shed old habits and excuses, take some time to visit that private place within you. Close your eyes and visualize yourself as being completely free of these limitations . . . how does your body react? If you feel good, that's all the evidence you need to prove to yourself that you have a rational reason to change.

If you're hanging on to a whole bunch of habits that have been reinforced by excuses, note that these will make you feel bad. Your old mental crutches only serve to keep you from having an experience within your body that registers as "good," so you may even be accustomed to being emotionally bankrupt.

Pain, anxiety, fear, anger, and the like make themselves known in your body as rashes, eczema, heart palpitations, arthritis, backaches, headaches, stomachaches, diarrhea, eyestrain, cramps, and many more ailments too numerous to mention here. The point is that these emotional reactions that show up in the body can become your way of life, to the point that they define your reality. And when you're questioning why that is, that's when the excuse *I've always been this way* tends to rear its ugly head.

You can feel better: You can feel healthy. You can feel strong. You can feel blessed. You can feel joy. In short, you can feel great! If the idea of eliminating an incapacitating thinking habit that you've had for a long time resonates with you, then imagine it being gone. Does its disappearance register in your body as a positive, healthy, and happy sensation? If so, then that alone is reason enough to plunge into the *Excuses Begone!* formulations presented here.

Criterion #4: It Must Be Aligned
with the Callings of Your Soul

How do you determine that you're aligned with your soul's purpose? You know by the way the rational reason speaks directly to you in that personal place within. The thoughts and feelings that surface tend to go like this: *This is truly who I am. By making these changes and eradicating these excuses, I will be living my life on purpose, fulfilling a destiny I came here to accomplish.*

I could go on and on here detailing the benefits that accrue when you connect to the callings of your soul. However, I'm going to suspend my desire to write and just let you know that in the next chapter, the sixth question in the *Excuses Begone!* paradigm takes off from this point. It takes you on a journey in which you will see how the universe itself begins to cooperate with you through the Law of Attraction, when your habits detach from the world of ego and align, excuse free, with your Source of being.

I'd like to switch gears here by returning to the story of my son Sands, which opened this chapter. As I already mentioned, this young man has had a lifelong problem with waking up in the morning, but he was ultimately able to create a rational reason to change his old self-sabotaging thoughts and eliminate the excuses that supported his bad habit.

Sands loves nothing more in this world than to surf in the ocean. He was given a surfboard at the age of four, and he immediately paddled out to where the waves were breaking, jumped up on his board, and surfed all the way to shore. All of us stood there dumbfounded as we watched that little boy ride his first wave like an expert. As for Sands, he was hooked—he's lived and breathed surfing ever since. It's like he connected to his purpose the moment he jumped on that board.

My son has an entire library of videos on the subject and regularly checks the surf reports all over the world. He dons a wet suit and goes into the water with one of his many boards, regardless of his location on the planet or any consideration of the temperature of the air or water. He studies waves like an ornithologist studies birds. It truly is his great passion. In fact, he just returned from a 16-day trip throughout the islands of Indonesia, on a boat that specializes in taking surfers to some of the greatest waves available on planet Earth.

Now, for the 16 days that he lived in cramped quarters on a boat with eight other surfers, Sands was able to wake up every morning before dawn. He'd be out in the water all day, well past dusk; stay up at night to talk with the other surfers about the waves they caught that day; sleep soundly until 5 A.M.; and repeat the same routine for more than two consecutive weeks . . . and he never felt tired. The same is true when my son visits me on Maui—if the waves are good, he no longer has a sleeping-in-all-day habit.

For my son, a rational reason to change is the notion that he's able to live in harmony with his passion. So let's review the four criteria for eliminating the excuses that travel the same path as the habit itself:

1. Sands has a rational reason for changing his habit that definitely **makes sense.** Maybe you or I would perceive riding waves all day in freezing water as absurd, but to my son, this means that he's able to be in a place where his strongest desires are in rapport with his actions. The waves are there, he is there, and he loves riding on those waves—so it all makes perfect sense.

2. Sands has a rational reason for changing his old habits that's also positively **doable.** When he's near the water and is free to surf, without any real responsibilities, he never says, "I can't get up," "It's too difficult," "It's not my nature to rise early," "I don't have the energy," or any of the other excuses he likes to break out when he's away from the ocean. When his friends call to confirm that they're going to pick him up at 4:30 A.M., his first response is, "Great!" Regardless of what time he goes to bed the night before,

he can be found in the kitchen at the appointed time, fixing a bagel and drinking his juice, excited and ready to go on an early-morning surfing expedition.

3. There's no doubt that being in the water and riding those waves allows Sands to **feel good**, and I equate this with God. As I wrote in Chapter 9, whenever we're enthusiastic about some-thing, that means we're tapping into the God within—feeling *good* is akin to feeling *God*. And when we're doing what we love and experiencing the passion that accompanies such moments, we're truly being guided by our Source.

I watch my son as he paddles out, as he rides his board, as he tells me his stories of the barrel that he rode, and as he watches his videos—there's a kind of seeing with a capital *S* that isn't with him at any other time. His concentration in studying the waves and knowing exactly when to pounce is like observing a cat concen-trate on potential prey . . . pure poetry in motion. It's his nature, and watching him in these moments allows me to see him in a totally new light. It is the same excitement I feel within myself when I speak before an audience or as I sit here in my sacred space writing these words that I hope will touch you and unborn genera-tions as well.

4. All of what I've written above (as well as what follows in Chapter 17) leads me to conclude that for Sands, a rational reason to change a long-held bad habit is that his early-morning journeys to the sea are moments when he's being called by Spirit to get up and be in harmony with the **callings of his soul**. I have no doubts whatsoever about this conclusion.

Suggestions for Applying the
Fifth Paradigm Question

— Do a unique inventory within yourself, an honest assess-ment of what lifelong thinking patterns you'd like to change, even if you haven't a clue as to how you could possibly bring this about. The more firmly entrenched the path in your mind, the better.

Now, without even considering how you're going to put this change into effect, ask yourself the first three criteria in this chapter and eliminate any that don't measure up:

1. If it doesn't make sense to you but everyone around you is telling you that it's the right thing to do, erase it from your inventory.

2. By being brutally honest with yourself, determine if, given the conditions of your life and how well you know yourself, this thing is truly doable. You may not know *how* to do it, but you can still assess if it is in fact something that's possible for you. If it isn't, then discard it.

3. Picture yourself as being free of your habituated way of being, totally disconnected from the habit. If that idea doesn't make you feel good—and I mean *really* good—then it's not for you.

Clean out the inventory of habits you'd like to break, and excuses you'd like to see vanish, based upon the criteria for having a rational reason to change. You'll be left with several lifetime thinking habits that make sense, are doable, and leave you feeling good.

Try putting one of the habits from your inventory to the test of the *Excuses Begone!* paradigm. After doing so, you might not even recognize the person you used to be. I know that when I think of some of the old habits I've freed myself from—such as drinking diet sodas, eating greasy foods, not exercising, procrastinating on deadlines, always being rushed, speaking out and talking over others rather than listening, not taking health supplements, being right rather than kind, and so on—I've noticed how much I've changed . . . and that those old tiresome excuses never seem to crop up anymore.

225

— Really examine your habits, along with all of the excuses you've adopted to explain yourself, and then ask yourself a simple question: *Do these make me feel good?* If the answer is no, then it's incumbent upon you to begin the process of making decisions that do in fact make you feel good. It's the same as aligning with the callings of your soul—because feeling good does indeed lift you into alignment with the callings of your soul.

Say this aloud: "I intend to feel good, and anything that I think or do that interferes with this intention must, out of necessity, be shelved permanently." You are allowed to feel good; it is your birthright. You emerged from the total bliss of oneness—God, if you will—into this human experience.

According to the Tao Te Ching, all being comes from non-being. I urge you to feel your innate goodness by eliminating the limitations that have kept you from experiencing the good feelings you had before beingness, and what you will have after beingness as well. Just stating, "I intend to feel good" is a powerful and rational reason for living an excuse-free life.

Use reason in eradicating excuses and habituated behavior. As Benjamin Franklin wrote in *Poor Richard's Almanac* in 1753: "When Reason preaches, if you don't hear her she'll box your Ears." Listen up or cover your ears!

CHAPTER 17

THE SIXTH QUESTION: *CAN I ACCESS UNIVERSAL COOPERATION IN SHEDDING OLD HABITS?*

*"The mystical techniques for achieving immortality
are revealed only to those who have dissolved all ties to
the gross worldly realm of duality, conflict, and dogma.*

*"As long as your shallow worldly
ambitions exist, the door will not open."*[3]

— Lao-tzu

As we move to conquer limitations, we're now going to switch from an intellectual approach to a spiritual one. Why? Because self-defeating habits, and their accompanying excuses, are the province of the ego, the part of us that has edged God out. Convinced that our identity is only of this earth, most of us are controlled and manipulated by ego's false interpretation of who we are. And as Lao-tzu reminds us in the quote above, as long as we're tied to shallow ambitions in the material world, we're going to continue to be slavishly tied to old habits.

When you ask yourself this sixth question: *Can I access universal cooperation in shedding old habits?* you begin to apply the mystical principles of higher consciousness to your life. Step-by-step, you dissolve the belief that you're exclusively tied to this material world. Even taking hesitant little baby steps will allow you to open the door to an amazing new existence.

Take a moment to review what your intellect has learned from the *Excuses Begone!* paradigm, and then trust that any help you need is forthcoming. When you completely relinquish the notion that you're separate from the mind of the universe—when you're in a God-realized or Tao-centered place—this is the point where you bid farewell to excuses.

Accessing Universal Cooperation

The moment has come for you to recover your original pure insight, the clarity and light that are within you now, as they always have been. *Enlightenment* means that you access that light within you, which is where you find Divine guidance. Now is the time to surrender your worldly ambitions and turn yourself over to that guidance.

The Source of all creation is pure energy, completely devoid of material form. You came from this Source, and you will return to it, as I've written frequently in this book. You don't have to physically die in order to access its unlimited power; you only need to become more like it. Your Source of being recognizes only that which it is, so when you're unlike your Source (or God, the Tao, the universal mind, or Spirit), that's when you're dominated by ego and think that you need all of its excuses. Yet Lao-tzu warns you at the beginning of this chapter that the mystical techniques for accessing Divine guidance cannot and will not be revealed when you edge God out.

Imagine a fish that lives five miles below the surface of the ocean: it has never seen light, has no experience of what air is, has no eyes, and thrives in an atmosphere so pressurized that it would squash any creature who lives above the surface. Now imagine that deep-sea fish communicating with a bird that's flying five miles above this creature's place of residence. You can see how unlikely this would be, since the sea creature can't recognize something that's in a separate reality system.

Likewise, your Source of being knows nothing of struggle, hatred, revenge, frustration, fear, tension, or excuses—these are all inventions of the ego. When you behave in ways that are separate and distinct from your Source, it can't communicate with you. Since conflict and excuses require duality, you can't access a Source that only knows oneness when you come to it in conflict or with excuses about why you aren't all that it intended you to be. In order to access the infinite power of the Tao, you must become more and more like God. In other words, you must move into the space where you experiment with thinking and acting like you imagine God does, and suspend your intellect.

The Law of Attraction proclaims that *like is attracted to like.* So when you think like the universal mind thinks, it will join you; when you think in ways that are antithetical to this Divine mind, you'll attract more of what you're thinking about. That means that if your thoughts are all focused on what's wrong, what's missing, what you can't do, or what you've never done before—that is, on *excuses*—you'll access more of what you're thinking about.

Use the Law of Attraction to say good-bye to excuses. When you do, the universe will recognize you, and help and guidance will show up in a synchronistic way. As you align with your authentic original self, rather than your ego, you'll start to feel as though you're collaborating with destiny.

Aligning with Source in Your Thoughts and Actions

If you attempt to figure out how your Source of being thinks, the first thing you need to do is get rid of the ego. When you observe how creation takes place, you see that Source energy is all about *giving,* while your ego is all about *getting.* So aligning with

Source energy means taking the focus off of *What's in it for me?* and shifting to *How may I serve?*

When you say, "Gimme, gimme, gimme" to the universe, it uses the Law of Attraction to say, "Gimme, gimme, gimme" to *you.* You subsequently feel pressured, put-upon, and out of sorts because so many demands are being made of you. It is out of this vortex that you create excuses that only serve to keep you stuck and striving to meet the ego's demands: *I'm not strong enough . . . I don't deserve it . . . I don't have the energy . . . I'm scared . . . It's too big . . .* and on and on. All of this stems from identifying with the false self that edged God out of your deliberations.

Shift to a new alignment now, one that puts you in rapport with the creative universal mind. You can begin by thinking like God, and follow up by acting like God. Take the focus off of *Gimme, gimme, gimme* and place it on *How may I serve? What may I offer? How can I help?* When you do, the universe will respond similarly, asking, *How may I serve you? What may I offer you? How can I help you?*

This is when the ego's old habits fall away and are replaced by unexpected meaningful events, with the right people, circumstances, and funding appearing. Lao-tzu comments on the magic of this practice:

> If you wish to become a divine immortal angel, then restore the angelic qualities of your being through virtue and service.
>
> This is the only way to gain the attention of the immortals who teach the methods of energy enhancement and integration that are necessary to reach the divine realm. . . . These angelic teachers cannot be sought out, it is they who seek out the student.[4]

The way to get to the point where you've abolished old habits and excuses is to petition the Divine realm and restore the angelic qualities of your being. Restoring is crucial, for when you begin to think like God thinks, you're actually returning to your Source of being without having to die.

I can't emphasize enough here that *you don't attract what you desire; you attract what you are.* Once again, I turn to Lao-tzu, who concludes the passage quoted on the previous page with:

> When you succeed in connecting your energy with the divine realm through high awareness and the practice of undiscriminating virtue, the transmission of the ultimate subtle truths will follow. This is the path that all angels take to the divine realm.[5]

That is to say that you can't just wish for a change, or simply think about what you want, and expect it to appear. To see the old habits fall away and access Divine guidance in making your life work at the highest levels of happiness, success, and health, you must *forget about what's in it for you.* Start practicing higher awareness by serving and wanting even more for others than you want for yourself. Otherwise, you'll never experience the subtle joy of a blissful, fulfilled life.

As Lao-tzu says, this is the only way. You can't demand guidance; it will come when you align as your Source is aligned. Then—and only then—as you live and practice the virtues, you'll gain the attention of the immortals. Otherwise, I repeat that the door absolutely will not open.

Living the Virtues

Some 2,500 years ago, Lao-tzu spoke of "the four cardinal virtues" and noted that when we practice them as a way of life, we come to know and access the truth of the universe. These four virtues don't represent external dogma, but a part of our original nature—by practicing them, we realign with Source and access the powers that Source energy has to offer.

According to the teachings of Lao-tzu, the four cardinal virtues represent the surest way to leave habits and excuses behind and reconnect to your original nature. That is, the way you were before acquiring physical form, and the way you will be when you leave your physical self. The more your life is harmonized with the four virtues, the less you're controlled by the uncompromising ego. And when your ego is tamed, you discover how easy it is to access Divine guidance—you and the Divine begin to operate on the same frequency. As you contemplate your life without excuses, you leave the ego part of you in the dust!

Below are the four virtues and how they manifest, along with a brief description of how they relate to your commitment to live an *Excuses Begone!* life:

The First Cardinal Virtue:
Reverence for All Life

This is number one because it is the key to diminishing the ego. The Source of being is the Source of *all* beings, including our planet and our universe, and it doesn't create that for which it has no reverence. Since the Tao or God is in the business of creating and allowing, why would it create anything that is unlike itself, or even worse, something that it despises?

To that end, the first cardinal virtue manifests in your daily life as unconditional love and respect for all beings in creation. This includes making a conscious effort to love and respect *yourself,* as well as to remove all of the judgments and criticisms from those early memes and mind viruses. Understand that you are a piece of God, and since you must be like what you came from, you are lovable, worthy, and Godlike. Affirm this as often as you can, for when you see yourself in a loving way, you have nothing but love to extend outward. And the more you love others, the less you need old excuse patterns, particularly those relating to blame. Excuses originate in a false belief that the universe and its inhabitants aren't there for you. The notion that they're obstacles—inhibiting you from living at your highest levels of success, happiness, and health—is based on an inauthentic premise.

As you adopt this first cardinal virtue, allow yourself to see others as willing to assist you in maximizing your human potential. The more reverence you have for yourself, and for all of life, the more you see everyone and everything as willing assistants, rather than inhibitors to your highest life. As Patanjali put it so succinctly several thousand years ago: "When you are steadfast in your abstention of thoughts of harm directed toward others, all living creatures will cease to feel enmity in your presence." The key here is to stay so steadfast that you seldom, if ever, slip from this first cardinal virtue.

The Second Cardinal Virtue: Natural Sincerity

This virtue manifests itself as honesty, simplicity, and faithfulness; and it's summed up by the popular reminder to be true to yourself. Using an excuse to explain why your life isn't working at the level you prefer isn't being true to yourself—when you're completely honest and sincere, excuses don't even enter into the picture.

The second virtue involves living a life that reflects choices that come from respect and affection for your own nature. Ralph Waldo Emerson described the significance of sincerity in an 1841 essay, *The Over-Soul:* "Deal so plainly with man and woman, as to constrain the utmost sincerity, and destroy all hope of trifling with you. It is the highest compliment you pay." And the great humanitarian Albert Schweitzer once observed that "sincerity is the foundation of the spiritual life."

Make truth your most important attribute. Walk your talk; that is, become sincere and honest in all that you say and do. If you find this to be a challenge, take a moment to affirm: *I no longer need to be insincere or dishonest. This is who I am, and this is how I feel.* From now on, when you make a commitment, do everything in your power to live up to what you've promised. Remember that when you're living your life from the perspective of your truest

233

nature, you connect to Source. And as Schweitzer said, this is the very foundation of the spiritual life. As you work at being totally honest with yourself and others, those old self-defeating habits no longer crop up.

When you know and trust yourself, you also know and trust the Divinity that created you. That means if you want to live in the mountains or by the ocean, so be it—you know it's your soul calling you to live harmoniously within your true nature. If you love sculpting and no one else gets it, so be it. If you want to become a triathlete, a ballet dancer, a hockey player, or a trapeze artist, so be it. If you live from honesty, sincerity, and faithfulness to the callings of your spirit, you'll never have occasion to use excuses. This is the significance of the second cardinal virtue offered by Lao-tzu, a mighty tool that you can employ as you work your way through the *Excuses Begone!* paradigm.

The Third Cardinal Virtue:
Gentleness

This virtue personifies one of my favorite and most frequently employed maxims: "When you have the choice to be right or to be kind, always pick kind." So many of your old thinking habits and their attendant excuses come out of a need to make yourself right and others wrong. When you practice this third virtue, you eliminate conflicts that result in your need to explain why you're right. This virtue manifests as kindness, consideration for others, and sensitivity to spiritual truth.

Gentleness generally implies that you no longer have a strong ego-inspired desire to dominate or control others, which allows you to move into a rhythm with the universe. You cooperate with it, much like a surfer who rides with the waves instead of trying to overpower them. I recommend that you look very closely at your relationships and find out how much of your energy is directed toward dominating and controlling, rather than accepting and allowing.

As you develop this virtue, the pronoun *I* ceases to be the center of your communication. Instead of insisting, "*I've* told you so many times how to deal with these frustrating and rude people," you're more likely to say, "*You're* really having a tough day. Is there anything I can do to help?" Beginning a sentence with "I" implies the need to control; beginning a sentence with "You," on the other hand, expresses kindness and consideration for the other person.

The more kindness and sensitivity you extend to everyone in your life, the less likely you are to blame others for not living up to your expectations. Gentleness means accepting life and people as they are, rather than insisting that they be as *you* are. As you practice living this way, blame disappears and you enjoy a peaceful world—not because the world has changed, but because you adopted this third cardinal virtue of gentleness.

The Fourth Cardinal Virtue:
Supportiveness

This virtue manifests in your life as service to others without any expectation of reward. Once again, when you extend yourself in a spirit of giving, helping, or loving, you act as God acts. As you consider the many excuses that have dominated your life, look carefully at them—you'll see that they're all focused on the ego: *I can't do this. I'm too busy or too scared. I'm unworthy. No one will help me. I'm too old. I'm too tired.* It's all *me, me, me.* Now imagine shifting your attention off of yourself and asking the universal mind *How may I serve?* When you do so, the message you're sending is: *I'm not thinking about myself and what I can or can't have.* Your attention is on making someone else feel better.

Anytime you're supportive of others, you automatically remove ego from the picture. And with no ego, you go from edging God out to being more like God. When you think and act this way, the need for excuses evaporates. Practice giving and serving without expectation of reward (or even a thank-you)—let your reward be spiritual fulfillment. This is what Kahlil Gibran meant when he wrote in *The Prophet:* "There are those who give with joy, and that joy is their reward."

The greatest joy comes from giving and serving, so replace your habit of focusing exclusively on yourself and what's in it for you. When you make the shift to supporting others in your life, without expecting anything in return, you'll think less about what you want and find comfort and joy in the act of giving and serving. It's so simple: no focus on yourself equals no excuses.

The four cardinal virtues are a road map to the simple truth of the universe. Remember what Lao-tzu offered you 500 hundred years before the birth of Jesus: "These four virtues are not an external dogma but a part of your original nature." To revere all of life, to live with natural sincerity, to practice gentleness, and to be in service to others is to replicate the energy field from which you originated.

Starting on the following page, I'm going to take you back through the list of the 18 excuse categories to see how they evaporate if you live the four virtues and consequently access universal cooperation:

Excuse	Accessing Universal Cooperation
1. It will be difficult.	With God, all things are possible.
2. It's going to be risky.	I cannot fail when I trust in the wisdom that created me.
3. It will take a long time.	There is only now. I live fully in the present.
4. There will be family drama.	My inner callings are the voice of God. I must follow what I feel so deeply.
5. I don't deserve it.	Everyone deserves the grace of the Tao.
6. It's not my nature.	My nature is to have reverence for all of life—to be sincere, gentle, and supportive to all.
7. I can't afford it.	If I stay in God realization, all that I need will be provided.
8. No one will help me.	How may I serve others so that they may have what I desire?
9. It has never happened before.	I am content with all that has shown up in my life.
10. I'm not strong enough.	I know that I am never alone. I will reach out to others who are not as strong as I am.
11. I'm not smart enough.	I trust in the Divine, omniscient intelligence to which I am always connected.
12. I'm too old (or not old enough).	In an infinite universe, age is an illusion—there is only now.
13. The rules won't let me.	I live by the four cardinal virtues.
14. It's too big.	If I can conceive of it, passion and the abilities to create it will be given.
15. I don't have the energy.	There is an energy in the universe greater than me, and that energy is always available.
16. It's my personal family history.	Everything that has ever happened to me was perfect, and I can learn and grow from it.
17. I'm too busy.	With infinite patience, I produce immediate results.
18. I'm too scared.	There is nothing to fear. I am an infinite expression of God (the Tao).

This sixth question in the *Excuses Begone!* paradigm is designed to assist you into a Tao-centered, God-realized pattern. As you've seen in this chapter, old thinking habits die quite readily when you get your ego out of the way and live by the four cardinal virtues. Without even trying, a need for defensiveness and justification disappears as soon as you reach out to others and take responsibility for everything that occurs in your life.

Suggestions for Applying the Sixth Paradigm Question

— Practice one of the virtues daily and take note of how it decreases your tendency to focus only on yourself. When you find yourself slipping back into an old, habitual way of being, use the moment to concentrate on unconditionally loving someone else. Then notice that the old thinking habits and excuses are no longer present.

Keep in mind that these four cardinal virtues represent the real you, the being you were prior to developing the false self (ego). Notice how naturally good you feel when you're demonstrating reverence for everyone, natural sincerity, gentleness, and supportiveness—that's because you're in harmony with your Source of being. All that it takes to remove an old self-defeating habit is returning to your original nature in the moment.

— Dissolve as many ties to the gross worldly realm of conflict and dogma as you can. Recall how Lao-tzu suggests that by doing so, you'll see the door open to universal cooperation. Stop identifying yourself on the basis of what you have, whom you're superior to, what position you've attained, and how others view you. See yourself as a piece of God, willing to act as close to that consciousness as possible. When you desire something, try wanting it more for someone else than you do for yourself; in fact, act to make it happen for them before you even think about yourself. Or if you're about to be critical or unkind to anyone, remind yourself that your original nature is gentle. Imagine yourself in a formless world about to transform into a material being—that state of nonbeing is who you were before you cultivated ego and began the process of edging God out.

The way to access universal cooperation in shedding old habits is to realign with your original nature in all of your thoughts. Think like God thinks, practice the virtues in all of your thoughts and behaviors, and devote yourself to living a selfless life. It cannot fail you. Your habits will dissolve and your excuses will surely be . . . gone!

CHAPTER 18

THE SEVENTH QUESTION: *HOW DO I CONTINUOUSLY REINFORCE THIS NEW WAY OF BEING?*

*"The mind is indeed restless, Arjuna: it is indeed
hard to train. But by constant practice . . . the mind in
truth can be trained. When the mind is not in harmony,
this divine communion is hard to attain, but the man whose
mind is in harmony attains it, if he knows, and if he strives."*

— Lord Krishna, from the Bhagavad Gita

When they're next to each other, the number 1 and the number 8, which is the symbol of infinity, signify one infinite Source. I invite the symbolic nature of the number 18 to inspire this final chapter of *Excuses Begone!* along with the last question of our paradigm shift.

In Hebrew, the number 18 signifies life. There are also 18 holes on a golf course, which can't simply be an accident, can it? The Tao Te Ching contains 81 chapters, and many believe that it was contemporaneously written with the Bhagavad Gita, the ancient Hindu holy book that just happens to contain 18 chapters.

The Bhagavad Gita details the conversation between Krishna, an avatar of the god Vishnu, and the spiritual warrior Prince Arjuna. The quote that opens this chapter comes when Krishna, who is disguised as a charioteer, gives advice to Arjuna as he's preparing to go into another huge battle. Elsewhere in this iconic volume, Krishna instructs: "Give not your love to this transient world of suffering, but give all your love to me. Give me your mind, your heart, all your worship. Long for me always, live for me always, and you shall be united with me." This is the essential message of *Excuses Begone!*

Unite with God, the Tao, universal mind, or Source; and trust in this wisdom, which is your original nature. Know your original nature so that you can intuitively turn your awareness away from this transient world when necessary. Then you don't need or want self-defeating habits or excuses.

Krishna reminds you that with constant practice, your mind can be trained to overcome any habits of thought. The key is *with constant practice,* and that's the affirmative answer to this seventh and final question: *How do I continuously reinforce this new way of being?*

Practice the essence of *Excuses Begone!* daily or even hourly, particularly the seven questions comprising the paradigm. When you do, before long you'll find yourself running those seven questions through your mind in a matter of moments—and you'll come out on the other side of an old habit with a new way of thinking, acting, and being. Learning to overcome excuses involves training your mind to become harmonious, or at one, with your Source. As Krishna says: "When the mind is not in harmony, this divine communion is hard to attain, but the man whose mind is in harmony attains it, if he knows, and if he strives."

The remainder of this chapter focuses on suggestions for staying in harmony with your Source of being. Thinking like God thinks is essential for all of your practice—not so much to learn new techniques for overcoming excuses, but to keep you consciously connected to Source and detached from the material world as much as possible. In this way, you'll let the angelic realm guide you through all of the doors that will now be opening for you.

Nine Ways to Reinforce Your New Way of Being

Throughout these pages, you've had the opportunity to examine the many ways your mind has learned self-sabotaging thoughts. You learned how those bad habits became a familiar reality system for you, with a catalog of excuses explaining why you abandoned your original nature in favor of edging God out. Now, however, you're freeing yourself of those excuses by training your mind to welcome and cultivate your original spiritual nature.

Each of the seven principles for living an excuse-free life, as well as the seven components of the new paradigm, are directed toward the message Krishna imparts to Arjuna: *When you get your mind into harmony with Source, there will never be a need for bad habits or excuses again.* As he states in the Bhagavad Gita:

> *Even the worst sinner becomes a saint*
> *When he loves me with all his heart. This love*
> *Will soon transform his personality*
> *And fill his heart with peace profound.*
> *O son of Kunti, this is my promise:*
> *Those who love me, they shall never perish . . .*
>
> *Still your mind in me, still yourself in me,*
> *And without doubt you shall be united with me . . .*

Here are nine suggestions for uniting with your Source, and living from that place:

1. Know It

As Krishna tells Arjuna, your mind can be trained if you *know* that you and your Source cannot be separated. This knowledge is so close—it's only a thought away.

Knowing is like having a private room that contains all of the answers you need, and only *you* have the entrance key. Since it's in you, you can go there at any time, and no one can prevent you from accessing what it contains. The moment your sense of knowing dissolves, however, old habits and a ton of excuses inundate you. When you're aligned with your Source, you're guided by the greatest good; without that alignment, your Source and guidance don't tend to get involved with the way you choose to live your life. Create your own space where you're aligned with Source, and then ego and doubt can't enter.

Always keep in mind that no single person, place, or thing can force you to believe or disbelieve anything. Perhaps that was true when you were a child, but not now. Now you have the independence to choose what you believe. Your knowing is *yours*.

Here's how I speak to myself about my own knowing:

> A sacred space is within me that contains a knowing. I go there frequently, and I don't allow doubt into that Divine inner dwelling. It is mine alone, and I share it with my Source of being. It is to this knowing that I retreat whenever I find myself slipping into excuse habits. In this knowing space within, I have no doubt about the guidance that's available to me when I'm unified with my Source. I know that the doors will remain closed and the angelic teachers will not seek me if I'm only attached to this corporeal world of conflict, material things, and judgment. I keep this knowing space sacred for the moments when old habits and excuses attempt to influence my life.

Be aware of how significant this doubtless knowing is for living an excuse-free life.

2. Act as Your Source Would in Every Instant

From this place of inner knowing where doubt is banished, ask: *What would God do right now?* (Or, if you conceptualize God as love, ask: *What would love do now?*) If you're ever perplexed by your habitual thoughts, asking this question will serve as a way to reinforce that there's an alternative. When you ask what God or love would do, you attract the Source energy that was lost in your voyage from childhood ego development to the present.

A few hours ago, the sound of a chain saw cutting a cement pole in half permeated my writing space, and my habituated way of thinking began to surface. I felt so resentful toward the noise pollution that I thought about quitting for the rest of the day, with the built-in excuse: *How can I write with all of this racket? It's their fault, not mine.* But I decided to reinforce the *Excuses Begone!* way of being by asking: *What would God do?* Then I sat down, dismissed my judgmental notions, and let myself be in peace. Within a few moments I chose to ignore the sound and write anyway, imagining the chain-saw noise as music to accompany me. Five minutes later, the noise was gone—and I'd sent an excuse packing by being in a God-realized space instead of continuing with an ego-dominated inner dialogue.

3. Initiate a Conversation with Your Habitual Mind

As you work to overcome your self-created limitations, talk to your subconscious, telling it that instead of *reacting*, you're now going to *respond* with conscious choices. This will work rather quickly for you if you're serious about breaking a pattern—awareness of feeling locked into automatic reactions, along with a serious commitment to change, will allow you to choose a new response.

This is what happened with my 30-year habit of drinking caffeinated diet soda. Until that day in 1985 when I chose to break this habit, I drank six to eight cans of carbonated brown water every day. I'd certainly been living at what I call the "reaction level," with excuses to explain and fortify why I did this, so I made a commitment to myself to change. I knew I wanted freedom from the chemicals that dominated my life so much that I was seldom without a can of them in my hand, and this became much more important to me than continuing down my well-trod path.

I became vigilant about noticing my subconscious pattern: as soon as I caught myself reaching for a soda, I'd stop myself and

245

substitute a conscious response that aligned with my commitment. By the same token, if *you w*ant to break a pattern, you need to truly commit, and then start conversing with your habitual mind. You'll be amazed at how fast the excuses disappear!

4. Get Quiet

Decide to reduce the noise level of your life. Noise is a distraction to your highest self because it keeps your ego on red alert. Ways to discard habits along with their attendant excuses are often found in silence, in the void that's the creative Source of all form. I've always loved Blaise Pascal's observation on this subject: "I have discovered that all the unhappiness of men arises from one single fact, that they cannot stay quietly in their own chamber." And *this* from a scientist!

Another scientist, Albert Einstein, reminds us of the importance of noise reduction as we become more adept at outgrowing the habits of childhood: "I live in the solitude which is painful in youth, but delicious in the years of maturity." Adopting a similar attitude will help you reinforce your *Excuses Begone!* life. So learn to take time each and every day for quiet contemplation: For example, when you're driving alone, turn off the constant chatter bombarding your inner world. Then when you arrive at your destination, honor the OFF button on the TV remote—and honor the ON button for your highest self!

Try to make meditation a daily practice as well, even if it's only for a few moments. (If you're unsure of how to begin, I've written a book called *Getting in the Gap* that comes with a CD to guide you in learning the meditation technique of Japa, which has been so extraordinarily helpful to me.) This is how Carl Jung described what he felt in deep meditation: "Those inner states were so fantastically beautiful that by comparison this world appeared downright ridiculous. . . . It is impossible to convey the beauty and intensity of emotion during those visions. They were the most tremendous things I have ever experienced."

Finally, while you're in that inner bliss-filled silence, let yourself be willing to simply ask. *A Course in Miracles* points out that you do not ask too much; in fact, you ask too little. And of course the Bible says: "Ask, and it will be given to you" (Mark 7:7). All creation stems from the void, the great silence—this includes the creation of a new you devoid of self-defeating thinking habits and accompanying excuses. As Swami Sivananda reminded his devotees: "Silence is the language of God." Ask in silence, listen in silence, and let silence be the jumping-off point for becoming one with the creative force of the universe.

5. Reenergize Your Surroundings

The Law of Attraction works when you surround yourself with people who are on a spiritual path similar to your own. Remember, this law states that like is attracted to like, so you attract Source energy to you by being like it. Similarly, when you're continually in the company of low-energy, angry, depressed, shaming, hateful people, you'll probably find life a little more challenging.

It was said of Jesus that when he entered a village, the population would be elevated just by his presence; no one could bring him down. Become more Christlike yourself by remembering that no one can bring *you* down because of his or her low energy. If people around you are angry or depressed and you feel drained emotionally, it's your responsibility to yourself to create the right energy for you—you don't have to join them in their negativity. Stay in your place of peace, regardless of how tempting it may be to lash out or argue.

Practice Lao-tzu's four cardinal virtues, and keep your environment as pure and free from negativity as you possibly can: Literally and metaphorically turn off any medium that broadcasts a litany of reasons to be depressed and frightened. Make your home a temple of kindness and love. Stay away from places that thrive on loud noise, alcohol consumption, smoking, and insensitivity. Pay attention to the music you listen to, the art you view, even the arrangement of your furniture and flowers—all of it! The more peaceful and loving your environment (and the people in it), the more you're in a serene place where excuses aren't on the agenda. This is the environment in which self-defeating habits are most likely to fade from your consciousness.

Further reinforce your new way of being by having your surroundings reflect the design of what you want your life to look like. In this energy, like-minded people will appear. Choose to be in the company of those who hold a space for you to achieve the joy of maximizing, rather then minimizing, your highest human potential.

6. Get Back to Nature

When I'm on Maui writing, I make it a weekly practice to drive halfway around the island to a lush spot with a stunning waterfall that empties into a refreshing pool, where I spend several hours swimming and meditating while the water cascades down on me. In those moments it feels as if God has entered my consciousness, and a rapturous feeling of contentment overwhelms me. This is a ritual I do just before beginning a new chapter, and it reconnects me to my Source of inspiration. There's no confusion, no worry, no fear . . . nothing but pure ecstasy and a lightness of being. In these moments, which I cherish deeply, I receive the answers I seek, not only for the writing I know I'll be doing in the next several days, but for my personal life as well.

This setting that showcases nature's beauty is pure God in action. As I get quiet and listen, any self-limiting thoughts are simply impossible. I understand what my spiritual friend Thoreau meant when he wrote these words in 1854, explaining why he chose to live in nature at Walden pond: "I went to the woods because I wished to live deliberately, to front only the essential facts of life, and see if I could not learn what it had to teach, and not, when I came to die, discover that I had not lived."

You will also find your answers in nature, because God *is* nature: unspoiled, untended, alive in stillness, and teeming with life. When you're there, you'll begin to see the miraculousness of every cubic inch of space. You'll feel the presence of an energy that you may have lost touch with in your daily life, and that energy is in you, just as it is in all of the flora and fauna. The creative spirit of God or Tao is so easy to align with when you're in a natural, unpretentious setting.

A week before writing this chapter, I trekked to the waterfall and natural pool with someone I love, stood in the cool flowing water, and ate guava fruit hanging from a branch above the surface. In those moments everything I needed to say here solidified. Excuses were out of the question, and I understood what Einstein wrote in his later years: "I lived in solitude in the country and noticed how the monotony of a quiet life stimulates the creative mind."

7. Practice Yoga

As I mentioned earlier in the book, the meaning of the word *yoga* translates to "union." The ancient *rishis* who gave us yoga considered stretching, balancing, and flexible exercising an opportunity to experience union with God. Such a union with the Source of being wasn't a painful experience, since God was viewed as natural, peaceful, and gentle.

In our Western world, the most popular exercise regimens involve some degree of harsh, vigorous, punishing, no-pain/no-gain activity. These include: running or jogging; bicycling; aerobics; and weight lifting, particularly on complicated machines, to add muscle tone. Yoga, on the other hand, has no harshness to it. Yet even as you stay in a space the size of a small mat, you attain the same kind of benefit those other physical pursuits give you, without the pain or exertion.

Yoga is a great workout for the entire body—particularly the joints, muscles, and even internal organs—but especially for the mind. I've practiced it just about every day for four years, and it's been a great healing factor in overcoming the aches and pains I inherited from three decades of daily running and weight lifting, along with the endless stopping and starting that accompanied years of competitive tennis. I lived with chronic back pain for many years before I began my practice of a daily 90-minute class of Bikram hot yoga, and I'm happy to say that I've been pain free now for almost four full years.

One of the most appealing features of yoga is that it's done in silence. The mind gets to stop all of its chatter and concentrate on union with God through specific *asanas* that are designed to align the body, mind, and spirit with the Source of being. And that's why I included this little pitch for yoga in a book on eliminating excuses and bad thinking habits—this entire work has been about finding a way to reconnect to the Tao in all of our thoughts and actions.

When you experience union, let go of your ego and no longer rely on excuses. In the 2nd century B.C., Patanjali, who is often called the father of yoga, defined it this way: "Yoga is the ability to direct the mind exclusively toward an object and sustain that direction without any distractions. . . . Yoga is the control of the ideas in the mind." Now this is precisely what an *Excuses Begone!* approach to life teaches. Control your mind, and everything will fall into place.

Give yoga an honest 30-day trial. Notice how your body feels better all over, and your inclination toward excuses dissipates as well!

8. Make Sure Your Number One Relationship Is with Your Senior Partner

I know that you have many significant and important relationships: certainly the ones you enjoy with your children, parents, spouse/lover/significant other, co-workers, and best friends rate very high in your life. Here in the *Excuses Begone!* paradigm, however, I ask you to place your relationship to your Source of being at the very top of this list. When this becomes your reality, you intuitively go to the silence within and remember to send your ego to a place where it doesn't interfere with your deliberations.

Make your relationship to Source your priority even if you declare yourself an atheist. When you go to this place within yourself, you don't need any religious orientation or belief in the supernatural. You needn't see God as a bearded old white man floating around in heaven awaiting your requests. You needn't believe in talking snakes; whales swallowing people and then spitting them out; God's only son being sacrificed by his Father in order to save us; or boats with all creatures on board, including insects and dinosaurs, to assuage God's wrath with a flood that covers the earth. While these stories are fine, I have my own opinions on religious tales, as I'm sure you do.

Rather, I ask you to think of God—or the Tao, Divine mind, Krishna, Source, or any of the thousand names for God—as love. Even the Bible itself states that "God is love" (1 John 4:8). And when Carl Jung was asked in an interview if he believed in God, he said these words, which reflect what I want to convey: "I could not say I believe. I know! I have had the experience of being gripped by something stronger than myself, something that people call God" ("The Old Wise Man," *Time*, February 14, 1955).

There's a loving energy in the universe that allows for the creation of all beings. It is a nonbeing without form or boundaries, and it does nothing while leaving nothing undone! Make this energy your primary relationship, above all others in your life, consulting it before anyone else. Retreat there in silence, and listen and know that this force is outside of you and within you. It's here that you will be guided to change self-defeating excuse patterns.

By all means, love your family (and everyone else on this planet). Treasure all of your relationships, but first and foremost make your relationship to your highest self your priority. When you see God simply as love, there will be no room left for excuses and bad habits. You will only be able to give away the love that is your creative essence.

I vividly recall reading an essay published in *Time* magazine that was written by Patti Davis, the daughter of former President Ronald Reagan, describing her long battle with cocaine addiction. She wrote that after she'd been clean for five years, the desire to take up the old habit was still very pronounced within her. She concluded her commentary by saying that although the desire was still there, and the memory of the euphoric feeling in her brain when she was on the drug was still enticing, she continued to stay away from this debilitating habit because she didn't want to disappoint God by returning to those old ways.

This is what it means to make your relationship to God the supreme relationship. It seems that Patti could handle disappointing her parents, her friends, and even herself, since she had done so many times. But she just couldn't go back to a state of being that was antithetical to Source energy, because her primary relationship in life was now to God. And in all honesty, I must say that this is the reason I personally have never gone back to alcohol.

As you can see, old habits disappear much more readily when you make your Senior Partner number one in your life. That's because your Senior Partner is pure love, and when you go there first, all that you could ever need is provided for you.

9. Work the Paradigm

I close this chapter with a reminder to work the *Excuses Begone!* paradigm whenever you find yourself stuck in self-defeating thought patterns or behaviors. The paradigm can be applied at any time, to any long-standing limitation that you want to change. When you notice that you've employed an excuse, just say these three words: *Work the paradigm.* In a matter of moments, the old mental crutches will vanish.

You can easily work the paradigm by quickly going through each of the seven questions and silently responding with short answers. When you notice that any question in the paradigm elicits a response that keeps the old excuse pattern activated, shift your answer so that it aligns with the highest vision that you have for yourself. This is a powerful act of changing the way you've allowed yourself to be conditioned to think, but it only works as long as you are honest and keep what you're doing a private matter between you and the highest part of yourself.

I don't feel that there's any need for me to elaborate on the seven questions we've already looked at in such detail. However, I would like to leave you with a brief summation of the essence of the *Excuses Begone!* paradigm, with a short response to each of the seven questions:

1. Is it true? *Probably not.*

2. Where did the excuses come from? *I allowed them.*

3. What's the payoff? *I get to avoid risks and stay the same.*

4. What would my life look like if I couldn't use these excuses? *I'd be free to be myself.*

5. Can I create a rational reason to change? *Easily.*

6. Can I access universal cooperation in shedding old habits? *Yes, by simply aligning with my Source of being.*

7. How can I continuously reinforce this new way of being? *By being vigilant.*

If you work the paradigm several times, you'll soon see where you're guiding your life with thoughts that aren't necessarily true. You'll be able to discern where those thoughts came from and what your life would look like without them, and then you'll create a rational reason to change them by accessing Divine guidance through perfect union with your Source of being. To be consciously merged into that perfect union with God is a feeling that's difficult to explain, but ego does take a backseat. You know that you're allowing yourself to be guided by a force that's bigger than you are, yet if you so choose, you can stay infinitely connected to it. In this state of knowingness, excuses become a thing of the past.

In 1851, Thoreau described his boyhood ecstasies in his journal, and his words take me back to my *own* boyhood ecstasies. I'm ending this very personal book with his observation because it is to those kinds of moments that I urge you to return as well:

> There comes into my mind such an indescribable, infinite, all-absorbing, divine, heavenly pleasure, a sense of elevation and expansion, and [I] have nought to do with it. I perceive that I am dealt with by superior powers. This is a pleasure, a joy, an existence which I have not procured myself. I speak as a witness on the stand, and tell what I have perceived.

I too perceive that I'm being dealt with by superior powers. I too speak to you as a witness telling you what I have perceived. I too have felt the all-absorbing, Divine sense of elevation that comes from living my life with a minimum of excuses. And as I conclude this labor of love, I wish for you to come to know the heavenly pleasure of living each and every day aligned with your Source of being in such a way that you can shout out: "Excuses, I no longer need you in my life, so be . . . gone!"

ENDNOTES

[1]From *Hua Hua Ching: The Unknown Teachings of Lao Tzu,* translated by Brian Walker (Harper San Francisco, 1992).

[2]Ibid.

[3]Ibid.

[4]Ibid.

[5]Ibid.

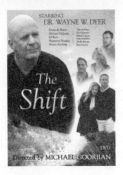

ABOUT THE AUTHOR

Dr. Wayne W. Dyer is an internationally renowned author and speaker in the field of self-development. He is the author of more than 30 books, has created many audio programs and videos, and has appeared on thousands of television and radio shows. His books *Manifest Your Destiny, Wisdom of the Ages, There's a Spiritual Solution to Every Problem,* and *The New York Times* bestsellers *10 Secrets for Success and Inner Peace, The Power of Intention, Inspiration, Change Your Thoughts—Change Your Life,* and *Excuses Begone!* have all been featured as National Public Television specials.

Wayne holds a doctorate in educational counseling from Wayne State University and was an associate professor at St. John's University in New York.

Website: **www.DrWayneDyer.com**

NOTES

NOTES

NOTES

NOTES

NOTES

NOTES

NOTES

NOTES

NOTES

NOTES

NOTES

NOTES

Hay House Titles of Related Interest

YOU CAN HEAL YOUR LIFE, the movie,
starring Louise L. Hay & Friends
(available as a 1-DVD program and an expanded 2-DVD set)
Watch the trailer at: **www.LouiseHayMovie.com**

THE SHIFT, the movie,
starring Dr. Wayne W. Dyer
(available as a 1-DVD program and an expanded 2-DVD set)
Watch the trailer at: **www.DyerMovie.com**

ALL YOU EVER WANTED TO KNOW FROM HIS HOLINESS THE DALAI LAMA ON HAPPINESS, LIFE, LIVING, AND MUCH MORE; conversations with Rajiv Mehrotra

THE BIOLOGY OF BELIEF: Unleashing the Power of Consciousness, Matter & Miracles, by Bruce H. Lipton, Ph.D.

FOUR ACTS OF PERSONAL POWER: How to Heal Your Past and Create a Positive Future, by Denise Linn

HEALING YOUR FAMILY HISTORY: 5 Steps to Break Free of Destructive Patterns, by Rebecca Linder Hintze

THE LAW OF ATTRACTION: The Basics of the Teachings of Abraham®, by Esther and Jerry Hicks

MIND PROGRAMMING: From Persuasion and Brainwashing to Self-Help and Practical Metaphysics (book-with-CD), by Eldon Taylor

RETURN TO THE SACRED: Ancient Pathways to Spiritual Awakening, by Jonathan H. Ellerby, Ph.D.

TRANSFORMING FATE INTO DESTINY: A New Dialogue with Your Soul, by Robert Ohotto

VIRUS OF THE MIND: The New Science of the Meme, by Richard Brodie

WHO WOULD YOU BE WITHOUT YOUR STORY? Dialogues with Byron Katie; edited by Carol Williams

All of the above are available at your local bookstore, or may be ordered by contacting Hay House (see last page).

We hope you enjoyed this Hay House book. If you'd like to receive our online catalog featuring additional information on Hay House books and products, or if you'd like to find out more about the Hay Foundation, please contact:

Hay House, Inc.
P.O. Box 5100
Carlsbad, CA 92018-5100

(760) 431-7695 or (800) 654-5126
(760) 431-6948 (fax) or (800) 650-5115 (fax)
www.hayhouse.com® • www.hayfoundation.org

Published and distributed in Australia by: Hay House Australia Pty. Ltd., 18/36 Ralph St., Alexandria NSW 2015 • *Phone:* 612-9669-4299 *Fax:* 612-9669-4144 • www.hayhouse.com.au

Published and distributed in the United Kingdom by: Hay House UK, Ltd., 292B Kensal Rd., London W10 5BE • *Phone:* 44-20-8962-1230 *Fax:* 44-20-8962-1239 • www.hayhouse.co.uk

Published and distributed in the Republic of South Africa by: Hay House SA (Pty), Ltd., P.O. Box 990, Witkoppen 2068 • *Phone/Fax:* 27-11-467-8904 • orders@psdprom.co.za • www.hayhouse.co.za

Published in India by: Hay House Publishers India, Muskaan Complex, Plot No. 3, B-2, Vasant Kunj, New Delhi 110 070 • *Phone:* 91-11-4176-1620 *Fax:* 91-11-4176-1630 • www.hayhouse.co.in

Distributed in Canada by: Raincoast, 9050 Shaughnessy St., Vancouver, B.C. V6P 6E5 • *Phone:* (604) 323-7100 • *Fax:* (604) 323-2600 • www.raincoast.com

Take Your Soul on a Vacation

Visit **www.HealYourLife.com®** to regroup, recharge, and reconnect with your own magnificence.Featuring blogs, mind-body-spirit news, and life-changing wisdom from Louise Hay and friends.

Visit **www.HealYourLife.com** today!

HAY HOUSE RADIO®

Take Your Soul on a Vacation!

Visit **www.HealYourLife.com**®, featuring blogs, healing news, and life-changing wisdom from your favorite Hay House authors.

Tune in to Hay House Radio to listen to your favorite authors:
HayHouseRadio.com®

For a complete selection of Hay House products, visit: **www.HealYourLife.com**®

Yes, I'd like to receive:

□ Information on the NEW Wisdom Community
□ Information on the NEW Women's Wisdom Circle by Christiane Northrup, M.D.
□ A Hay House Catalog
□ The Louise Hay Premier Online Newsletter
□ The Sylvia Browne Premier Online Newsletter

Name _____

Address _____

City _____ State _____ Zip _____

Phone _____

PLUS, if you give us your e-mail address, we will e-mail you a $10 coupon good for your online purchase at: **www.hayhouse.com**!

E-mail _____

To:

HAY HOUSE, INC.
P.O. Box 5100
Carlsbad, CA 92018-5100

Place
Stamp
Here